Poetry 2010-2024

Poetry 2010-2024

Reflection Of Self

Kyaira Harjochee

Published by Kyaira Harjochee, 2024.

REFLECTION OF SELF

First edition. May 12, 2024.

ISBN: 979-8224608843

Written by Kyaira Harjochee.

Table of Contents

Middle School Woes

Thank You Veterans

(6th grade- my first poem)
Very eager to come home
To enter and return to all their homes
See how much America has changed
Tonight, the troops are coming home
Thanks and cries come from far and near
"Welcome home" brings a lot of tears
Some are here, others are gone
Tears of happiness and others sadness
Thank you for bringing freedom home
To all that are here
Thank you, Veterans, for bringing us hope
And a reason to try
Thank you very much for all the help
For bringing freedom to our nation.

Without Me

I want to be so much more than you can see
But how can I be happy
Without someone to love me.
Yet you say there's a way.
But for me it's never ending,
So I'll just wait.
Maybe one of these days,
When the world turns round,
I'll figure out what love is about.
Then I hope I can find my destiny,
Love is different to you and me.
'Cause I don't see you,
And you don't see me.
I don't know how you see my friends,
But not me.
So as I rock myself to sleep,
I wonder what the world would be,
If you didn't know me?

Would These Feelings Ever Go Away?

Was she not beautiful? Was something wrong?
Wrong with her?
He said he didn't like her, Didn't like her because-
Because she was a "nerd"
He didn't want her, He didn't like her,
Were they still friends?
That is what she wondered,
And as she thought of what he said a tear fell down, Her world spun
around,
Her world felt like it was crashing down all around her, She liked him for
what seemed to be many years,

But he hadn't felt the same,
And this is when she cried, Cried silently,
Every tear all her feelings,
She didn't attempt to hold them in, She let her tears out,
Within this all her questions were answered,
And in this she cried, Cried for him.

Rage's Inner Pain

Just Trust

One minute they trust me the next they don't.
Drugs?
What?
Depression? It's you.
Give up friends?
(Not gonna happen),
I won't give up any more for you.
First you trust me,
Now you don't?
We're close,
Or at least that's what I thought.
Don't put limitations on myself?!
But WAIT!
You're the one limiting ME!
You want me happy?
Then let me live free!
I have my morals and values set straight.

When will you see?
I'm not you and I'm not her!
Stop trying to stop me from making the same mistake you all did.
I see what it caused,
I see what it did.
Just trust me,
Just have a little faith.
If you really loved me, you would give me a chance,
A chance to prove,

There's a meaning,
There's a point-
TO WHAT I'M DOING!
Yes,
I know you only care,
But care enough to let me learn from MY OWN MISTAKES.
Everyone deserves a chance.
Will you just trust me?
When I say I trust them.
I'm not throwing away friendships because you say I can't!
I KEEP YOUR SECRETS!
I NEVER TOLD!
HE STILL DOESN'T KNOW!
I thought at least you would have my back.
It hurts more coming from you,
Yeah, someone else I would expect it,
But from you,
I never saw it coming.
And will you just stop for a second and realize,
EVERY TIME I do something YOU DON'T LIKE YOU say I'M JUST
LIKE HER!
I'M NOT!!!
I'M ME!!!
NOT HER!!!

The Anger of My Youth

Society calls it mommy issues-
A mother who made you feel alone in life
Society calls it daddy issues-
A father who raped you as you cried in
pain

The thought of every breath you've ever breathed enrages me-
You are the source of the anger of my youth.
I loath you-
The way you are who you are.
You're existence is the Bain on mine.
I what to scream until the vibrations makes your head explode,
I step on cracks in hopes all of your bones break,
I whisper words in the wind in hopes they consume your soul never to let go
until you acknowledge and mean an apology for what you did to me.
I don't want to hear the story of how your pulse falls flat–
When you think back to all the pain you caused-
You've proved that statement is only an excuse.
I could never hurt my children,
I could never allow pain to come to my children without fighting to my own
death to stop it.
So how were you okay with what you did,
What you allowed to happen to me?

Dear M.F.o.a.M (My Failure of a Mother)

To my failure of a mother
I don't care if you play the victim card
I don't care if you say I caused you pain by turning you away
I don't care if you sit alone at night crying out your eyes
I don't care if you live alone and die with no one at your side
To my failure of a mother
Where were you when I needed you
Where were you when I wiped the tears from my own eyes
Where were when I was a child fighting for my life
To my failure of a mother
I don't care how you feel
I don't care if your heart ever starts to heal
I don't care about your pain
I don't care to see your face or ever hear your name
To my failure of a mother
Will you ever take accountability for the pain you put me through
Will you ever see what's wrong with you standing up for my abusers
Will you ever listen to my voice and attempt to heal the wounds of mine
that you made fester
Will you ever acknowledge the hell you put me through the hell you let me
suffer through
To my failure of a mother
I felt alone in my pain
I felt alone even if you were in the same room
I felt alone when there was no answer as I sought you out for comfort
I felt alone every moment of my life that your presence existed in
To my failure of a mother

It was your job to protect me
It was your job to stand up for me
It was your job to fight for me
I wasn't suppose to be alone
I wasn't the one who failed you
You failed me
Dear my failure of a mother
But don't worry I learned from your failures
So Thank you my failure of a mother for teaching me the kind of mother I
never want to be
The kind of mother I rather die than ever be
Goodbye my failure of a mother it's time to close the doors and windows
time to lock you out for good
Don't knock
Don't call
Don't speak mine or my children's names
You lost that freedom when you made my children cry
Just know those tears of theirs were the first and last that will ever be caused
by you
You will not put them through what I went through
You'll never have the chance to make them question their importance
I promise you my failure of a mother you'll never get the chance to be their
failure of a grandmother
Todays the day I erase your name from my family tree
I'm done allowing you to continually fail me
You'll never fail me again
You're no longer my failure of a mother
You're just a failure of a person
a name without importance
You can have all the memories back I don't need them anymore
Don't bother to remind me of your name I'll never use it
Don't bother to spill lies of loving me because I've never felt it
Go live your failure of a life
Here's your trophy
You came in first place for best example of the person no one wants to be.

Your Actions

Your actions taught I'm not allowed to hurt
Not allowed to release the pain you caused.
You taught me you're the only one allowed to be upset,
The only one allowed to hurt.
I don't care if you paint me as the monster in your story,
You don't have to be painted to be seen as the monster you already are.
You're a monster in the story of my life,
You're a monster that stands behind my hurt- my pain
That I have yet to find a way to erase.

A Father of Pain

There's something about you I just don't like,
There's something about you that crawls up my skin.
There's something about you I just don't understand,
There's something about you that makes you worse than other men.
There's something about you I just can't place,
There's something about you that waves red flags in my face.
There's something about the devil in your eyes,
There's something about how you smile when I cry.
There's something about the evil between your teeth,
There's something about the chill left when we meet.
There's something about you that smells like death,
There's something about you that feels like a lack of justice.
There's something about how you laugh at other's pain,
There's something about the lies you serve on silver plates.
There's something about an evil soul,
There's something about the way you say my name that feels like whips and
chains.
There's something about a man that should be a ghost,
There's something about a mortal with no soul.
There's something about a father who causes pain,
There's something about you that seems will never change.

Siren Song

Hear my siren song
My voice beckons from beyond
Step into the sea
Let the waves crash into thee
Calling you to come find me
As I call to you it is now time for you to meet your doom
Step into the sea
Let the ocean consume thee
Hear my siren song
As it draws you towards me
Feel the pain you have caused as you step into the sea
May my salty tears sting your lungs as you fight for air
May my salty tears burn through your skin as the waters hurl you into the
ocean's depth
Hear my siren song
'Tis time to meet your doom
As the waves bury you in your ocean tomb
Hear my siren song
My voice beckons unto you
Drawing you into the waters to meet your doom
Never again will you bring torture or pain
'Tis the time for the ocean to take you away
Feel the pain you've caused
Hear my siren song
You killed the child inside me
With every bruise every scar
You slowly killed me

Every time you took advantage of my body
You slowly chipped away at my innocence
Every time you called me a "pretty girl" as you tucked my hair behind my ear
And told me it wouldn't hurt for long
You killed the child inside of me who wanted to be seen
The child inside me who once had sought beauty in their self
Every time you beat me
Every time you would rape me
You slowly chiseled away at the child within me
You slowly killed me
You killed me
But I've been reborn as a siren to stop you from inflecting these same pains
again on anyone
I've been reborn
Hear my siren song as it calls from the beyond
Drawing you into the sea
With waters unforgiving
'Tis the time of doom
For this sea made of salted tears to consume you
To fill you with the agony you once inflicted upon us
'Tis time for you to be buried beneath the ocean's floor
As the waves hurl you into your ocean tomb
Hear my siren song as I call into the wind
I wish not an easy death but instead death from within
Though you seek death you shall never find it
The spirits I call friends shall inflict on you the same agony you inflicted
upon us
You will wish for death but now you're cursed
Cursed to live in constant agony
How can you call yourself my father when you threw me into walls
You put your hands around my neck,
Wrapped your arm around my only connection to air,
Slowly suffocating me
How can you call yourself my father when you beat me until my skin turned
purple and caused blood to seep out of me

How can you call yourself my father when you threw hammers from across
the room barely missing me
How can you call yourself my father when you cursed my very existence
Screaming telling me you bet I wasn't yours
Did telling yourself that make it easier for you to justify to yourself the
cruelties you inflicted upon me
How can you call yourself my father when you lie straight to my face
You said if you knew what your father's girlfriend did you would have
stopped her
Yet in the records as a child I stated you were sitting by the bed laughing as
she inserted the handle of that metal fork inside my first grade body
You were sitting in the room when she stopped what she was doing to me to
do it to my younger siblings
You were sitting in the room you could have stopped it but you didn't
Instead you sat there laughing because somehow you got pleasure from our
pain
How can you call yourself my father when it took me years to retrieve my
childhood memories just to find the child inside of me hiding in a
shadowed corner curled up afraid to leave afraid to talk to anybody
How can you call yourself my father when you're responsible for the
shattering of my psyche
How can you say you love me when it's clear you never have
How can sit back and expect me to want you in my life
I don't want to be connected to you
Or have your blood coursing through my veins
I don't want to be your daughter but that's something I can't change
Every bruise, every scar, every time you chipped away at my innocence as
you took advantage of my body
You killed the child inside of me
You drove her into hiding
That child died many years ago
But from her ashes I have arose
I have been reborn
I now stand to bring down you or anyone who inflicts such agonies
And now it is time for you to finally hear me

Hear my siren song
Step into the sea
Let the waves crash into thee
Hear my voice
I now speak out
You cannot escape
You now must face what you have done
The pain, torture, and agony you have caused shall now be turned back
tenfold on you
Hear my siren song
Hear my pain
Hear the child you beat and raped
Hear the child from inside me whose innocence you slowly chiseled away
HEAR MY SIREN SONG-
As the waves hurl you into your ocean tomb
Never able to escape the agony that shall consume you.

Siren Of Old

My spirit is not new to life
My spirit sees what it must fight
I sense the vile thoughts in your mind Within your human form a monster
lies
What evil fills you past your brim
What malice lives in you
I see the thoughts circling your mind
I feel the pain that you have caused
What terror you've inflicted upon innocence
With hate the monster in you spreads it's wings and takes flight
My spirit sees you for your truth
A monster that you cannot hide
Who I was in my past life
And who I'll be in my next
The siren of old in a body of new
I call out to you
the monster in disguise
The monster you hide inside
I'm here to consume the evil within you
The ocean of sorrow will be your tomb
Answer my call for your time is up
You cannot hide the truth
You cannot disguise who you are from my eyes
Who I was my past life
Who I'll be in my next
The siren of old in a body of new
I call out to you

the monster in disguise
The monster you hide inside
Cannot flee from me
I will devour your evil and send you body below the waves
It's time the monster within you meets its final day.

Pages of lily

18

In Search of Lily

I search through the petals of memories-
In search of my dear Lily-
A valley full of petals-
But a flower only you
Lily, have you seen her?
Or did she wilt away?
The petals are beginning to fade away
Someone please tell me have you
Seen Lily?

Ode to Lily

There once was a girl named Lily,
She held all my secrets.
Only one knew her name 'til they told my parents.
Then my parents yelled and shamed me-
Saying Lily wasn't real.
They told me to stop making up names,
And that's when Lily left.
She went deep into my mind to hide from everyone,
But after she left my parents could not stand who they said I had become.
They knew Lily-
She was the good little church girl who always held her tongue.
Lily who was never bothered-
Lily, who broke herself just to take the weight off of everyone else's shoulders.
They complained that I had changed,
What they did not see was that I was still me.
But it was Lily that they loved-
It was Lily they wished were me.

A Child's Day Is a Mother's Memory

Life grows over the hills Where children play and sing
While dancing and laughing the cherries blossom on the trees,

The wind sweeps through the meadows and ripples spread across the river
Where fish jump and children swim and laugh
While living and loving the day within the day.

When the night falls and stars light the sky
The children run through the tall weeds and grass in pursuit of lightening
bugs.

In the distance the voices of loving mothers begin their journeys across the
plains,
And children say goodbye to their friends until the day next,
And they go running and skipping home to be tucked in and kissed a top
the head
After their favorite stories had been read.
Mothers flick on their children's nightlights and turn off the one keeping
their children awake
As they go to crack the door,

They grab the jar of blinking lights and whisper a sweet goodnight,
Then go out of the room and step outside to release the flying lights for the
next night's hunts.
With this the mothers, Each in their own homes,
Sit out on the porch and think upon the beauty of their every day And their
love for each child.

Run Until Tomorrow

Running is like flying
Once you start you don't want to stop,
But then you have to because of the curse of tiredness takes over.

Running, it well, accelerates the body, Puts the mind in the back seat.

Any problem can be removed shortly by running,
When you run you runaway your problems and they don't come back until
you stop.
So, I say "Run"
Run as long as your heart provides a beat And as long as every step carries a
melody, Run until your lungs can no longer hold air.
Run and Run and Run.
Run into tomorrow because tomorrow never comes.
Today we look and run into tomorrow, But when we reach tomorrow it's
today, So, we just keep looking and running.
So again, I say,
"Run and let your feet carry you away".
Tomorrow will never come,
So, keep running in search of tomorrow,
It's the only way to forget the problems of today.

We Are Grass

Some say the grass grows taller on the other side, Some say it grows brighter.

But I say every blade of grass is different yet the same.

Just as each blade of grass grows at its own pace and some never get cut
down while others get cut,
But those that are cut down each are cut by a different blade, At a different
angle,
Never exactly the same as the one before it.
People are like blades of grass, Some grow tall,
Some are cut down,
And some are constantly being cut down.
If the lawn is to grow
If the world is to be made brighter and better

THE GRASS HAS TO GROW!
People mustn't be cut down!
Let life expand and spread As is wild grass and flowers.
We are grass And
We are flowers.
We are living,
But are we thriving?
Stop mowing the minds that are expected to better the world.
Let the people be grass.
Let children remain flowers that make the grass glow and grow.

"The Water"

Do you see the waters rising?
Do you see them becoming still?
Do you feel the waters coming up from within?
Do you taste the words the water places on your tongue?
Do you know what the water represents,
Do you know?
The Spirit that flows from the Creator into their Creation,
Do you know that's the water?
Drink up!
I say to you- if you are weary,
If you are thirsty
The Water will free you of this world.
Do you remember the waters that comforted you in your mother's womb?
The Water,
The Spirit,
Has been with you since the Creator began their Creation of You.
Do you know-
Do you see-
Do you feel-
Do you live in step with-
The Water?
The Spirit is with you
Will you drink the water of wisdom?
Will you eat the mana of the heavens that fall like rain waters?
Will you accept the Water as your own?
Take the Water & let the Water take you.

"The Answer"

My mind wonders-
But peace takes hold,
I've prayed and prayed-
And it seems as if the answer has been received,
The answer has been revealed.
Peace is the answer I've been waiting for,
god's stillness is also an answer in & of itself.
Peace is 'yes this is the right one'.
god's stillness is a 'wait, it's not the time yet'.
So as my answer is revealed I become aware of what is to be done,
I am to wait with them,
Because they are the one.
And the one will wait if the voice I hear is the voice I feel,
And the voice I see inside of me.

"Feathers"

To think of feathers falling
I think a slow beautiful life.
To see the feathers falling
I see the heaven's gates open.
To find the feathers that fell
I find life, happiness, promises that last for eternity.
To picture feathers on a being
I picture angel wings a' glow.
If only I may touch a feather
If only I may lay my head upon a mound of feathers,
I would be touching something heavenly
I would be laying to rest in the arms of an angel.
To think-
To see-
To find-
To picture-
To touch-
Feathers
Would be to think
To see
To find
To picture
To touch-
Feathers.

"If I Were A Bird"

If I were a bird what would I do?
Would I fly?
Would I sleep?
Maybe crow?
Would I walk?
Would I run?
Where would I choose to make my home?
Would I nest in a forest or a top a human's dwelling?
Would I have the power to paint a picture?
If I were a bird what would I do?
Would I think before?
Maybe after?
Would I think at all?
If I were a bird could I hear god's voice louder?
Would god still talk to me?
Would god still guide me?
Would I have a purpose to fulfill,
If I were a bird?

Angel Wings

Do they carry you away?
Do they hide you?
Do they protect you?
-from the world-
Is it the thought of having a guardian angel that saves you from the world?
Is hope found on angel wings?
Is faith held on the fleeting wings of angels?
Does love come on the fleeting wings of angels? Does life become more on
the wings of angels?
Why is it the wings of angels bring us comfort?
What is it about angel wings that bring us a sense of peace?
Please tell me.
Why angel wings?
Or
Is it simply the angels themselves?
The world can't tell me.
So, you tell me.
What is it about Angel Wings?

With You in Paradise

I saw the sun blossoming over the horizon
And felt my heart rising with the light
And my soul longing to be with you,
My whole being aching to be where you are,
To be with you in Paradise.

The Levithan's Lamentations

Of lapis lazuli she's made or so her color seems-
Her name is Lam as Lamb-
Named from which I first react of her precious blue stoned
coloring.
But she reminds me of someone-
No something-
The Levithan!
So many run from her in fear-
For she has knurling snaring teeth
And oh the strength
To crush them with just the look of the eye.
But I cannot help but stop and stare-
Because her beauty is severely rare.

Truth

When I thought I was beyond saving-
You saved me.
Though I feel I don't deserve it-
You give mercy-
You show me glory
(Your glory).
Every time I fall you're the one who picks me up
& helps me to walk to safe ground.
You bless me everyday
I don't always realize it but its true-
You're the Truth.
My Truth.

Unchanging

No matter what I do you're always there-
When I fall you're there to catch me-
When I think I've fallen to far you pick me up-
No matter what I do you're always there-
When I turn from you and rebuke your name-
You're still there-
You still love me-
You're unchanging-
No matter what I do you're always there-
You're always there-
It doesn't matter what I do-
Or what I say-
You still love me-
You're unchanging-
No matter what I do you're always there-
You always will be-
Unchanging.

Strength & Love

You stand in the distance,
You walk with me-
Even when I'm unaware of your presence,
You never leave-
Even when it feels like you have,
You never push yourself onto me-
You give me freewill to make my own choices,
And when I call out you reach out-
You mend the broken pieces-
You lift me up-
You hold me in your peace,
And when I try to do the same for others-
The ones who believe & those who don't-
You guide me onto the path in which you wish for me to turn upon,
And when all is said & done-
When the only choice left is to say goodbye-
You give me the strength-
You show me it's what love would do-
You hold my hand-
You catch my tears-
Give me strength-
Show me love-
And then with your Strength & Love
I tell them Goodbye.

Only You Lord

Lord renew my heart-
Renew my soul-
Make me new in you.
You give me life beyond what I could imagine-
You answer prayers-
You open doors-
You help me conquer my fears-
You make me strong-
You hold my hand-
You guide me to where I need to be.
Lord renew my heart-
Renew my soul-
Make me new in you-
You make my dreams come true-
And I thank you.
I thank you Lord.

Beginning to Understand

Why you would do this for me I don't understand-
You gave up your only son so I may live forever-
I've sinned against you and you continue to forgive me-
You continue to love me,
Just the way I am-
Why you would do this for me I don't understand-
And all you ask of me is to do the same-
To forgive those who hurt me-
To love those who you love-
To love everyone and accept them for who they are-
Because you do this for me every day-
Why you would do this for me I don't understand-
At times I doubt you-
At times I give up-
You stand by my side and never leave-
You walk with me through the dark-
You're the only light in those times-
And you guide me to where I need to be-
Even after all I have said-
I have done-
Why would you do this for me I don't understand-
Why-
Why-
Why you-
Why you-
Why you would do this for me I don't understand-
I give up-

Because all I want is for you to walk with me-
I need you-
I need you-
I need you to guide me to where I need to be-
As you walk with me-
As you guide me to where I need to be-
I begin to see-
Why you would do this for me-
And I begin to-
Understand.

Salt & Light

You call me salt
And at times when I feel as if nothing more than a grain
You give me hope
You show me light-
You show me I am the light-
You give me the power to heal,
You give me all I need to be all you want me to be.
You comfort me-
So I may comfort others.
You gave me life-
So I may help bring life to others.

Timeless Value

"There is a time for everything, and a season for every activity under the
heavens"
-Ecclesiastes 3:1

The clocks tick-
Though we know not when the hands will hit the time-
Mere seconds and hours
Tell not what we are to know-
But counts until the proper season comes-
Until the savior's face we will behold.
We sit under heaven waiting-
Waiting for heaven to unite with earth-
And for the clock's faces to no longer hold value-
For with the arrival of heaven
Hearts hold all value-
Because heaven exists as timeless-
With no clocks,
Only opportunities
And perfect seasons-
Designed by our perfect Creator.

Cry of the Nations

God's voice is oh so loud
And it calls from above the clouds
I feel ropes
One standing still
While the other is trying to pull me back
As I take a step towards the rope in a tight grasp
The other begins to be yanked yanked yanked
And I see God's light
It's oh so bright
I step closer and the other rope yanks me towards the dimming nations
And these voices I hear
This voice I hear
The voice of the creator
The voices of the nations
The voices of the nations crying out
While the voice of the creator is calling out
'If only they'd open their eyes
If only they'd open their eyes & hearts & minds'
And the nations just sit back and cry not realizing God is waiting
Waiting:
To wipe away the tears he's catching
To heal the hearts he's been slowly mending
To takeaway unpleasant thoughts
Yet the nations cry out for only themselves
While God calls out for all of them to stop looking within themselves
Because the answers cannot be found within themselves
Only through him can they be found

'So child let God wipe away your tears,
Erase all of your fears,
Give me your heart and it will be healed'
God is calling out
But who is listening?
'Children stop crying,
Stop crying,
Rejoice in what you already have.
Rejoice because I have not forsaken you.
Though you have forsaken me,
I will not forsake you,
I will wait for you'
God calls out over the nations
His whisper is loud if only you'd listen.

The Blessings in the Stars

In years past I've tried to count the stars,
But I've learned-
If you try to count the stars you always have to restart,
But I've also learned-
If you start counting stars don't stop-
Because every star is worth more-
No represents more-
Then a billion blessings-
So to stop counting stars-
Is to stop counting blessings-
And that we are told to never do.
So count the stars-
As if-
Your blessings depend on it.

Drop in the Water

Drop in the water
Rush in the stream
Don't know where I'm going but
I'll let the water lead
Don't know where the steps I'm taking will lead me
But I'm gonna follow the current of the rushing stream
Drop in the water
Rush in the stream
Don't know where I'm going but
I'll let my lord lead
Don't know where he wants me
But in him I still find peace
Drop in the water
Rush in the stream
I won't worry as long as the water leads
The water rushes but takes slow steps with me
I know the spirit can be found in the rushing of the stream
Drop in the water
Rush in the stream
I'm gonna keep my focus on my lord who leads me
Drop in the water
Rush in the stream
I'm gonna go to my lord for cleansing
I'm gonna let go of all that's hold'n onto me
And I'm gonna let the stream carry me off
Drop in the water
Rush in the stream

I know the lord is with me
I know he'll never leave
Drop in the water
Rush in the stream
Let the water rush over you as you drop everything
Your past,
Your problem,
All your mistakes
Let them be washed away in the rushing stream
So...
Drop in the water
Rush in the stream
The lord is waiting to give you peace...

Inward not Out

Hope can be uplifting,
Hope can wipe away your tears,
It can change your life,
It can wipe your slate clear,
Open up your eyes,
Open up your mind,
Don't shut yourself down,
Don't shut others out,
Think happy thoughts,
Enjoy everyone; enjoy everything,
Don't doubt yourself,
Don't let the world knock you down,
Keep your head high,
Keep your thoughts in line,
Stay grounded to the ground,
Staying where you are isn't always the best option,
Be careful what you do,
Be considerate of others,
Just be yourself,
And never change for other people,
If you remember and do all these things,
You it will find,
And find you it will do,
Hope is like a dream,
For so long it just seems to always be out of reach,
Hope is not external,
Hope comes from within.

In-between Memories

I know what they say is true,
I couldn't have stopped what happened to me and you.
I was just a little kid,
It wasn't my fault they did what they did.
I was told I need to pray more and change how I feel,
God will help me heal.
And as I grow older,
I become more afraid but yet bolder.
When I was little I was afraid to wake up and go to sleep,
With there being no in-between my feeling of fear ran all too deep.
When I would close my eyes I would relive my past,
I would feel everything I used to feel and it would blow through me like a
cold winter's blast.
It's been three years since I've come out from being dormant,
And my life has been lit.
Time is flying,
And being happy is something I'm no longer trying,
Because I am and always will be happy right here with my family.

Don't Wait

Don't wait,
Don't wait for people,
Don't wait on people,
Don't wait on time,
And don't wait for the right time,
The right time is just an excuse not to take the chance-
Not to take a chance.
By waiting we're letting blessings slip out of our hands.
We're missing the big picture,
We're missing out on life.
They say we live and learn,
But when will we learn not to wait?

Belief is to the Belonging

I cannot make one believe in what I believe,
For religion- faith-
Is found within,
As answers to the soul's belonging,
Which in my eyes-
The world can dim-
But as we see every day-
Just as I believe in God-
Others find what they're looking for as they step outside their doors,
Answers exist-
You just have to believe to find them.
And if you believe-
Either you'll find the answers-
Or the answers will find you.
But I cannot make you believe what I believe.

The Vinedresser

"I am the true vine, and my Father the vinedresser."- John 15:1
You adorn me with the riches of your love
And protect me from the evils of this Earth.
I am yours-
So do what you will with me-
Use me as you see fit,
I give all I have to you
To be made into who you made me to be,
I give it all up-
I give it all to you
To be with you.
I am nothing more than a vine
Trailing this land-
But you are the vinedresser
Covering me with your wonders.
You gave me new beginnings,
You show me mercy,
And
You guide me along the path of
The righteous.
As I walk these narrow roads
You help me keep my eyes
On the path you have laid before me.
You proved the strength I need to be who you want
Me to be.
You are in me
And you shine through

With everything I do-
When people look at me
I don't want them to just
See me,
So I do all I can to make
You seen in me-
'Cause I am nothing more than a
Vine-
But you are the vinedresser.

Only One

"The King is not saved by his great army; a warrior is not delivered by his great strength." -Psalms 33:16

No one can save anyone,
There is only one who
May succeed,
Only one with the strength,
Only one without weakness,
The only one with enough love,
The only one without hate,
To bring us together
On our knees,
The battle is waging,
But it's
Already won,
We are all- in him,
He saved us and still
Does today,
He delivers us from all that overwhelms us,
Unlike men he can and does save and deliver everyone who comes to him.

Not to that of this World

"Thou shalt have no other gods before me." -Exodus 20:3
You may ask me where my loyalty lays-
To "my" country?
To "their" country?
To people?
To man?
To this land on which we all live?
You may tell me I have my loyalties mixed up-
Because mine may be different from yours-
But my loyalty does not belong to this land on which we live-
Neither does it belong to man/people-
"their" country or "mine"-
Nor will it ever-
Because-
My loyalty is to only one-
My loyalty is to whom-
Created this land-
Pieced together man/people-
United "them" and "us"-
My loyalty lays with the ruler of Heaven and earth-
My loyalty lays with the Lord-
It shall never lay with the World nor its Followers.

We (You) Will Be

"And the earth was without form, and void; and darkness was upon the face of the deep. And the spirit of God moved upon the face of the waters. And God said, Let there be light: and there was light." -Genesis 1:2-3
So many times we feel as if we are nothing-
As if part of us is missing-
As if we'll never be whole-
As if we'll never be worth anything-
As if we're nothing more than dust and dirt-
As if we're nothing more than that of this earth-
As if we're no better than what this world has become-
As if we're just slowly fading away-
But don't forget we were made from more than dust and dirt-
We were given life by God-
A God bigger than this world-
And in Him-
We will be Something-
We will be Void less-
We will be Whole-
We will be seen as precious Jewels-
We will be More-
We will be a Light in the Dark-
We will be bright as the stars Never Fading-
All you have to do is trust Him-
And allow yourself to see-
You are More-
You are Loved-
You are Precious-

You are Someone's World-
You are Everything to Him-
So to Him
And
Forever You Will Be.

He is Waiting

"And if it seem evil unto you to serve the Lord, choose you this day whom
ye will serve; whether the gods which your father served that were on the
other side of the flood, or the gods of the Amorites, in whose land ye dwell:
but as for me and my house, we will serve the Lord." - Joshua 24:15
Though we might pray for the Lord to change people-
He will not-
For He gives us freewill,
And though so many feel He is not present in their lives-
Because they do not feel He is searching them out-
He is here-
He does not need to search you out-
Because He has already found you-
He's just waiting for you to find Him-
He's just waiting for you to search Him out-
To come to Him with all your worries-
With all your burdens-
He is waiting for you to lay it all down-
To let Him take it all off your shoulders-
To let Him bring you peace,
But never will He force you into anything-
Because He loves you enough to let you make your own decisions-
To be your own person-
And He is waiting for you to love Him back-
Because you were His decision-
And He chose to love you-
And now He is waiting to be your decision-
And for you to choose to love Him.

Made to Return

"And the Lord God formed man of the dust of the ground and breathed
into his nostrils the breath of life; and man became a living soul." - Genesis
2:7
Our body was made of this-
Of the earth,
Our soul was given to us-
In a breath,
Though our body will someday return to which it was created from-
This being the dust of this earth,
Our soul shall return to that of whom gave us first breath-
This being the Lord in Heaven,
Though we were made of this world-
Our connection to the other I stronger-
For our body becomes one with earth once more and our body does not last
forever,
But-
Our soul returns to the Heavens and our soul does last forever,
This being how the Lord created us,
Good-
To help-
To be whole in Him-
Is what the Lord made us to be,
We were created in His image-
And given His breath-
So one day we may return to Him whom chose to create us.
This being how the Lord created us,
Good-

To help-
To be whole in Him-
Is what the Lord made us to be,
We were created in His image-
And given His breath-
So one day we may return to Him whom chose to create us.

In a Time of Trouble

"Is any among you afflicted? let him pray. Is any merry? let him sing psalms."
– James 5:13
Those who are hurting-
Who are afraid of tomorrow-
Who wonder why?
Who ask for understanding-
Those whose hearts have become bitter-
Fall-
Fall to your knees and pray-
Pray for tomorrow-
Ask for understanding-
Pray that your bitterness will seize,
Cry out with all you are-
Let Him know of your afflictions-
Pray for His help when you are troubled-
And praise Him for all the good He has done-
And all the good He will do-
Do not let your heart become weary-
Rejoice so you may be renewed in Him-
Give Him all you hold within so He can heal your hurting and restore your
joy-

Be not afraid to come to the Lord-
Be not ashamed of what you have to question-
Be not silent with Him for He will help if you only ask-
So find somewhere to kneel and lift your voice and hands-
Let Him back in-

Let Him help again.

58

I Dream

When I sleep-
I dream
Vividly- Colorfully
Peacefully- Frightfully
I dream-
When I sleep
Of yesterday
Today
Tomorrow
And forever
When I sleep-
I dream
Of people
Places
Things
And desires
When I dream-
I sleep
Of Missions
And children
When I sleep-
I dream
Of marriage
Of a future seen and created by God
When I dream-
I sleep
In hope

In love
When I sleep-
I dream
With faith
With happiness
I dream-
When I wake
Of seconds
Minutes
Hours
Days
And years to come
When I wake-
When I sleep-
I dream.

Cardboard Paper

Grief and I are no strangers
We stand hand & hand
When I rise he pulls me back down
&
When he goes under I pull him up-
We balance each other.
He finds me in my weakness,
And I find him at rest in my strength,
We complete each other,
He helps soften my heart.

Wake up from the Brokenness

When I awake and stand
I find myself staring at an empty bed,
Which reminds me of all the empty dreams,
Everything that seems so unseen,
The world is so full of brokenness,
And people blame it on loneliness,
If they could only see the broken pieces could be pieced together with one choice,
And all they'd have to do is listen to the calling of god's voice,
But the world does its best to sustain the pain,
Yet in the end it's not about our brokenness or our loneliness,
It's about the lives god will gain,
With the end of this world's raining pain,
But for now we're stuck-
Living in a world who's focus is self gain-
The change comes with us-
So step up-
Rise up-
Wake up-
Be the change-
Be the difference-
Don't wait for someone else to lead the way,
'Cause christ is the only one you need to follow
And he already set the way-
Paved the way of your future-
Our futures
Don't wait on the world-

Because it's to broken and unable to piece itself back together.

63

Ripples in the Water

So I guessed right shouldn't I be glad,
There's not really any reason to be sad.
Do I believe,
Or out my ear let her words leave.
It bothers me not,
I figured this much is what I would say I got.
So confusion fills my head,
Endlessly horrid dreams find me in bed.
Nightmares are supposed to cause fear,
But it seems they became too near,
To the paint I see the pictures clear.
Don't get this mixed up,
Her words are not the cause of my nightmares,
My lingering thoughts of "what could have beens"-
Keep me awake through the night.
But through these two inner mingled stories
I find myself in the midst of glory.
I have found a new friend-
Truly a gift from above-
Who helps me find peace.
And through what others would see as a bump in the road-
I see as the pavement of one of god's greatest gifts.

The Rest

They say this how I cope,
Me cutting off the ropes,
How much harder can it be,
I'm doing my best to hide the sorrow filling me.
AM I Broken or just worn?
My heart for sure is torn,
He's five years old,
He only knows what he's told.
I'm hoping if I stay away long enough maybe he'll forget me,
Maybe it won't hurt so bad when each other we can no longer see.
He's my baby brother,
But since he was born I had to take care of him like a mother.
I can't see him if we're only going to be separated,
I can't see him and let go of him every time we visit.
It hurts and it's all caving in on me,
Caving in on the inside,
I do my best to hide it,
I do what I can to fight it,
The pain seems to go away but then-
It comes back.
When I close my eyes-
They're all memories,
Sometimes I think it would be better if they were just dreams-
If there were no chance of them being reality-
No chance of being my reality.
It's confusing and sometimes I don't understand,
I don't get why all this happens.

But sometimes I guess it's best just to leave it,
Leave it in god's hands-
To do the rest.

66

A Teen's Internal Chaos

67

Flashbacks Unforgiving

These flashbacks play before me, all around me,
They play the same way they were created-
Uninvitedly
Like the people from across my past starting as a child-
The ones who made me feel like something worth nothing more than a
cheap toy,
A rag doll,
Something for them to play with then cast away,
Their hands where they were never meant to be,
Their "tools/weapons of their choice" being used against me along with
their words and laughter,
Their eyes seeing places and things supposed to be sacred to me-
All the while my mom away at work unknowing to the circumstances,
Unknowing to the to the threats of death to be caused if I told,
The monster in the chair across from the bed who watched and laughed
when they should've saved me-
Me,
A child merely six or seven,
The years blur together between things that I remember and memories that
I should have but don't,
The memories of sharing a bed with a monster head coated in red curls and
skin covered in speckles of brown-
The monster had a name "Misty",
To most just a descriptor of weather but to me a spiral of things I wish I
couldn't remember,
First it was me and then every in age below mine,
Forced to watch unable to close my eyes that they forced me to keep open,

Nearly twenty years of blaming myself to finally realize no matter what I wish I could have stopped the day my innocence was taken I was still only a child.

69

What's Behind The Mask?

This is my mask, This is your mask,
This is what breaks the mask,
Eyes are windows into the soul,
Can you see through my windows,
Do you see what's behind the mask,
These crystal orbs show more,
So how much more can you see in me?

That Day

That day I cried,
And reach me he tried,
I yelled and screamed,
And that's when I seen,
That hurt look on his face.
I never meant to be mean,
I just didn't want him to see,
See me crying,
Crying like it was all over.
But after he left Suli found me,
And we talked and talked,
We shared our stories,
She helped me end my tears,
That day we got close almost as if best friends.
And I'm sorry if I frightened him.
I learned a lot through that,
I learned a lot that day.

To Be Forgotten

At first they told me to forget,
Then they told me I need to remember and figure-out,
They said someone told them something,
What was said?
What is it that I don't remember?
Knowing the one who told what was told,
It's probably something my mind hid well,
And if so it was hidden for a reason,
The one who told has always disliked the one needed to be forgotten,
Remember what?
Remember why?
I don't remember,
So do I really need to,
Or can I just leave it alone,
And maybe wonder later.

Some Days

Some days I want to die
Some days I just want to cry
Some days are better than others
With this pain I hold inside
The reason why I cry
I want it flowing down my skin
A warmth that seeps out from within
Every drop of blood carries the weight of all my pain
If I could just let it out
It would run freely from my veins
I rather have my pain around me on the floor forever staining
But it's locked inside of me
Stuck in a constant pattern
Traveling through my veins and back up to a heart that has mostly shattered
The pain of emotion makes me long for something different
No emotions just numbness
Wondering why I have to feel
Some days I want to die
Some days I just want to cry.

Reaching Out

He speaks,
Filling the air we breathe with lies.
When we question what's going on,
He refuses to answer-
Sitting in silence-
Never making an effort to try.
We try to reach out-
But instead of connecting with him we connect with a wall.
How can we help him-
When he won't let us in?
How can we understand-
If he speaks no truth?
So many love him-
But you can see he still feels alone.
What can we do?
How can we reach him?
The only thing I know is Love more and more,
Never less-
And one day he'll realize just how greatly he's been blessed.

Not Feeling the Thoughts

A free land-
So full of life-
Yet, so alone.
He, this young boy,
Sits alone-
in a place-
on a rope and wooden swing-
Under a hidden tree-
Staring down at his own little toes-
As daddy plays with rowdy goats-
"Why does daddy spend all his time with the little goats?"
The boy asks his only friend, himself.
Out beyond the trees-
No, really, surrounded by the trees
A little farm lies-
In a tall grassy bed of yellow and green.
And behind the two hiding trees rests a cracking house-
With a slanted roof and broke windows.
The only brightness is off to the side-
A little red doghouse.
The leaves blow in the wind-
As the old man dances with his goats-
And a little boy forgets-
He has a difference to make-
A world to change-
Because he feels forgotten and alone-
Not quite sure if his house is really a home-

The land is a forest green-
Surrounding envy and solitude
If only the boy knew just how important he is-
The impact on others he'll make during and with the living of his life.
But for now the young boy doesn't know how to explain what he feels,
His thoughts have yet to hit his mind,
So for now- all he knows is- he is sad.

Questions and Answers

When you feel like you're drowning how do you swim?
How do you find who you are when you forgot everything
about yourself?
How do you fix things that seem unfixable? How do you feel when you're
numb?
How do you separate day from night when everything just blurs together?
How do you find the words to say when you have no words left?
How do you Love when Love is your greatest fear?
Why do people say "I'll help you" but when you go to them,
they say you have to figure it out on your own?
How do you find the answers when you're
asking all the wrong questions?
How do you know which questions will find you the answers?
What if the answers are in front of you and the questions are but the
answers in disguise?

Asking Why?

As I drift in and out of reality
I can't decipher my dreams from reality
My world spins
The lights dim
The Earth beneath me caves in
I see everything around me begin to fade
The images I see when I open my eyes are grey
But when I close my eyes-
The life behind my lids become colorful and vivid-
The paths in which our lives entwine leave us
asking why?

Why These Memories

Why does life always come in blows?
Why is when your scars start to heal, they are once again opened up?
When people are supposed to disappear,
Why do they all of a sudden reappear?
She was supposed to leave,
She was supposed to stay away,
Get out of my life,
So why is she back?
I don't want her here,
I don't care how much time she gives me;
I will never want her in my life,
I will never love her,
I can't stand her or who she's with,
I don't care how much she's "changed",
She's not welcome to come back into my life,
She'll never be part of my life,
Why is she calling now?
Why does she want something to do with US (no) ME now?
It's been like a year,
So why now,
when she's no longer on my mind?
Does she have to be here?
Why can't she just disappear?
I was perfectly fine,
Then she came back into my life,
I knew something would go wrong yesterday,
I could feel it,

And now I know,
I know what's wrong,
what was going to go wrong,
This,
the part of my life I hate,
She is the part of my life I hate,
Both of them;
I want them gone,
I want them out of my life,
Out of my life FOREVER!!!
I just want them to GO AWAY!!!
I want my memories of them to FADE!!!
I wish I didn't know them,
I wish they were never born,
Maybe then I wouldn't be this,
I know now I wouldn't have part of them in me,
I wouldn't be THIS,
THIS THING,
THIS THING I HATE!!!
Why does my life (no my past),
Eat me from the inside out?
Why is it half the time I feel dead inside?
Why am I so afraid to be myself?
Why am I afraid of pain?
So afraid of rejection of being hurt,
of not being loved of wanted,
Why am I?
Why did life happen how it did?
Why does she have such a big impact on me,
When she starts trying to come back?
Back into my life?
Why can't she stay gone?
I can't see him 'til I'm eighteen,
So why can't it be the same with her?
Why do I feel this way?

Why do I feel so broken?
Why do I feel like my insides are being ripped apart?
Why?
Why is it so hard to move on?
Why can't everything be erased?

Erased like the messed-up lines of broken art,
Why can't I erase these feelings?
Why can't I just forget?
Why can't I just go numb?
I spend a week in total and utter numbness,
I felt nothing,
Every day blurred with night,
I didn't like it,
I had no words,
No art in me,
But I didn't feel the pain either,
After the numbness went away,
I felt everything I had been hiding from,
Why can't it disappear?
Why can't these memories fade,
Why can't they dissolve,
Why do these memories hang on so tight?
Why can't she GET OUT OF MY LIFE?
Why can't she get out and STAY OUT OF MY LIFE?
I don't need her,
I don't want her,
I CAN'T STAND HER!!!!

Why?

Why does rain only sting fresh wounds
Why does pleating rain leave scars within
Why?
Why do I feel like I'm drowning inside
Why does love always hurt so much
Why?
Why care
Why breathe
Why?
Why do we only see the bad in ourselves
Why do we always push those away who truly love us
Why?
Why haven't I realized it before brokenness is brokenness and once broken
always broken
Why did I think someone would want to stick around after they knew the
deepest underlying cause of my own brokenness
Why?
Why do I love hard
Why do I love deep
Why?
Why can't I give up on others when they've already given up on themselves
Why does everyone think they know what's best for me, what I want, what I
need
Why?
Can anyone answer me this?

Dance To Go?

Today I woke up to wondering,
Wondering of what the day might bring.
So far so good or at least I think,
I'm just writing down my thoughts in fading ink.
So I talked to mom about a dance,
And when I asked if dad would let me go she said there was a pretty good
chance,
Now my only dilemma is who to ask,
Not knowing who to go with makes this quite a challenging task,
I think I'll just go alone anyways,
Here alone is how I've gotten used to living my days.
So what to do about the dance, I don't know.
It always baffles me at how things turn out.
How friends come and go,
But yet there are always a few who stick around.

Without Questions

Sometimes I wonder why my release is through words,
Sometimes I wonder why it's so hard to cry,
Sometimes I wonder why I am how I am,
Sometimes
- just sometimes-
I wonder about everything in general.
But each day I realize something different,
I learn a new lesson-
I make a new friend-
I start to see things more clearly-
I start to figure things out,
I start to stop asking why-
And I see just how happy my life can be-
Without questions surrounding me.

"My Nightmare"

Face to face,
We met Last Night,
As I fell into deep slumber.
My eyes were shut,
My mind was open,
The dream I dreamt,
Was quite a scare,
It showed me,
My worst fear.
That little girl,
She hit me once,
She hit me twice.
Then I swore,
And again she hit me,
Then I dragged her out,
By her hair,
I swore once more,
And gave her one last chance,
To turn around and walk,
But she jumped,
And yanked my hair,
Then she hit me a fourth,
And I slammed her in the ground,
I then calmly turned around,
She stood back up,
And lunged at me,
She grabbed my hair,

And tried to throw me,
On the ground,
Then once more she hit me,
My eyes flashed red,
My temper flared,
I threw her across the yard,
I then blacked out,
And I jumped on top of her,
I beat her,
There were screams,
And first one tried,
To pull me off,
Then another,
But I wouldn't budge,
Then they both,
Yanked me back,
They took me in the house,
And tried to take me out,
Of my rage,
But it wouldn't work,
So they poured cold water over me,
I then snapped back,
They asked me,
'What do you remember'.
I said,
'She hit me for the fifth time,
I swore at her,
And that's all I remember'.
They then took me to see,
What I did,
To that girl,
'I didn't do that',
Was what I whispered,
Then they confirmed,
That it was true,

I caused that pain,
I than screamed 'NO!',
And I ran outside,
I went and hid,
I began to cry,
They came out to retrieve me,
I screamed at them,
To stay away,
'NO, STAY AWAY FROM ME,
I DON'T WANT TO HURT ANYONE',
But they came closer,
And then I ran,
'No, I'm not going to-
Be close to anyone,
I don't want to hurt you,
Please, stay away'.
Is what I screamed.
They tried to catch me,
But I was too fast,
It seemed I was flying,
As I swiftly climbed the tree,
To get away.
Face to face,
We met Last Night,
As I gently shut my eyes,
The dream I dreamed,
It showed me,
My worst fear,
It showed me,
As a monster.
My worst fear,
Is me,
Myself on the other side,
My worst fear came alive,
In my Nightmare.

The Damage of Our Inner Monsters We Hide

As i realize this throbbing pain i feel comes from within-
I feel my insides start caving in
As the world dips and spins,
blurring the picture of life I see streaks,
like a movie watched too many times
As black static feels life's screen everything starts to feel so surreal Life's
nightmare coming back all too fast
Almost lost it
Almost become the monster hiding on the inside
Right under the surface,
Just waiting to be exposed,
Waiting to show the world who I am
The curse that runs through my veins
The blood staining my insides
Who they said i would always be
Who i've always been afraid to be

The monster inside
The secret troubles i have hid
Come alive before my eyes
Then i realize they are shut
A mere perception of life's undealt hands
Thoughts of what could've been
The lies and deceit that has forever held us back from grace
Our worries and fears we can't seem to let go of
But yet, we can still feel the salty stings of our tears

Hard to believe we are all somehow emotionally damaged
Whether it occurred in the past or present.

89

In A Short Time

Now you call me this,
You call me a whore,
You call me a slut.
You don't believe me,
When I say I didn't do drugs,
When I say I didn't have sex.
You don't trust me,
To pick my own friends,
To pick the right guys.
You think I made the same mistake as you,
I didn't,
He wasn't a mistake.
You say I need to be me-
I need to be myself,
I am but you didn't like me,
I am but you try to change me.
And yet you don't get it-
you don't understand,
No matter what is said THIS IS WHO I AM!
I WON'T CHANGE for you,
If I change it will be for me,
But I LOVE WHO I AM,
I'M HAPPY with WHO I AM.
I don't need you to like me,

You said yourself-
"Only a couple more years",

Just look at that,
A couple more years and if you still don't like who I AM You Won't Have
To See Me.
Everyone deserves a chance,
And no one should have to change for anyone
So just remember we don't have that long.

Just Like Me

Days blur into night,
Things seem to get better than worse.
I close my eyes in hopes that this reality is all a dream.
I guess I still wish things would have worked out.
I guess I still hope that one day they'll come back,
One day they'll tell me they're sorry,
Sorry for making me grow up so fast,
Sorry for not telling me they love me,
Sorry for making me afraid to open up and be myself,
Open up and let myself love and be loved.
Sometimes I still wonder,
If they really did ever care,
If they really did ever love me,
And if they didn't love me how could someone else.

But I'm glad to say I now know who I am and though others say this isn't
me,
It is and I know and I'm happy with who I am,
I'm happy at how far I've come,
through all that's happened I'm not like them,
I'm just like Me.

The Broken Tree- the broken me

Sorrow is just a word for sad,
And sad is known as the color blue,
And sorrow and sadness are often seen as a person who's broken too.
There are many ways to be broken,
For me it's mentally,
And sometimes my brokenness is in my heart,
And broken can mean sorrow
Or broken can feel empty,
Either way broken is pain and cracks and no way or no one to shield you
from the rain,
Earthquakes crack you,
Lightening burns you,
Floods freeze you,
But you don't feel it because BROKEN IS NUMB!

BROKEN IS NUMB
AND NUMB IS DEPRESSION!
To want to feel wanted,
To want to feel important,
To want to feel loved without a doubt,
But not to feel this leads to depression, I guess...
But they led me to self-doubt...
Am I not enough?
Did I mess up?
Is something wrong with me?
Why do I let myself feel this way?
And yet...

Somehow... This... is all my fault... SOMEHOW.

94

My Tears Are Different

Some people ask me why I don't cry-
And my answer is I do-
I cry on paper-
My words are my tears-
All my emotions are expressed in lead,
My emotions can be read,
Fear, anger, sorrow, sometimes happiness-
Is all laid out before me-
On my paper in grey ink.
I love my tears-
With each one is an endless memory.
Everything that stains my veins can be seen by my tears.
I express everything,
I tell my life story-
Through a waterfall of tears.

And though they can't always be understood,
They always mean more than anything else I could express in any other way.

A Porcelain Field

I have learned how to stop the seas from submerging a porcelain field of
agony-
Where the sun doth shine through clouds of grey-
And winds doth weep in the midst of a hollow grave-
As so solemnly flowers begin to welt away-
And this mortal casing corpse is turned to dust-
And the inner being returns to the nostrils of its creator-
It is here a beautiful picture of distress enters through the searching lens-
In which takes in-
But only releases what is willed to stop-

In fear of distorting a porcelain field.

The Hurting Waters

The wind still blows,
But the raging seas have seized,
Long years I have waited for this day,
But now I realize this day was postponed-
By no other than I,
I would not let the happiness seep through,
I had felt I was undeserving,
Like somehow all that has happened was because of me,
Like if I held onto humanity my life would last forever.
I thought I could make right what was done wrong,
I felt if I gave up my happiness that those I love would gain what I had lost.
So many times, I cried to be loved-
To be seen yet invisible-
To never be hurt again-
But I refused to open my eyes and realize I was causing the pain-
By not doing anything to stop what was happening,

When I realized-
When I stopped living a fantasy-
When I stopped and opened my eyes-
When I decided to do something about the pain-
It seized, just like the calming of a raging sea.

Tornado Inside

A breeze blows through me-
Bringing every memory-
Every thought along with it,
I struggle to escape-
But the air around me tightens-
The wind wraps every particle of its being around me refusing to let go,
Refusing to let me be set free-
Free from my memories-
Free from old fears-
Free from myself,
The earth forcing me to face myself-
To face memories-
To face fears-
To face the world I've seen-
The world I've heard,
The branches-
The trees-
Wrap their arms around me and refuse to release,
"You must face yourself- you must face who you are"
The wind howls in my ears-
The sun leaves me to the mercy of the sky,
As the clouds hurl rain and lightning at me-
The thunder booms-
The lightening blinds me momentarily,
Then the wind spirals around me-
And with it shows all my memories and fears,
And with it is life,

My Life,
The emotions and rage I hide inside-
Every fear I've ever hid-
Every thought I've ever had,
Every memory-
From every moment-
Every second I spent wondering-
Every second I was lost,
Every time I looked in the mirror-
And asked-
Who is staring back,
As the world breaths me in-
Like there is nothing else left in the atmosphere-
Like I'm its air-
I begin to feel,
I begin to feel-
Everything I forgot-
Everything I locked away,
I feel the pain-
I feel the hate-
I feel the torture-
The rejection,
No space-
No room to breathe-
No more life-
No more fight left in me,
The feelings fade-
The wind dies down-
The memories vanish for now,
I remain paralyzed-
Emotions run high-
They are no longer locked inside-
The wind released everything,
Then I feel life return-
Air forces its way into my lungs-

I feel damaged-
And broken-
But I'm still alive,
I take one more step-
I save one more life,
These feelings don't end-
They live on inside,
The wind gave me life-
The wind ended mine-
Then the memories-
The fears-
Were placed in my hands-
As I flipped through my mind's albums-
The memories-
The fears-

Flashed before my eyes,
And with it-
The wind brought back-
The feelings-
The pain,
In me-
Inside-
My emotions ran high,
I lived through-
My own-
Tornado Inside.

The World Today

Beating hearts
and
Pounding feet

Searching eyes
and
Screaming teeth

Lying lips
and
Drowning dreams

Broken homes
and
Shattered scenes

Heaving Lungs
and
Crying Souls

Unhinging Fists
and
Words never told

Unspoken Thoughts
and

Pain Foretold

Streaming Tears
and
Flowing Blood

Darkened Skin
and
Wounded Love

Pressing Bruises
and
Cutting Deep

Attempting Escape
and
Attempting to become Unseen

This is the World Cold Cruel
And to so many a
Defeat

But nothing is happening
or
So, people make it seem

As they forget
above
the lives ending

Violence, Torture,
and
All sorts of Pain

Crying children
And
making death a game

Shooting guns
and
Shooting up

Popping pills
and
Doing drugs

Not remembering
the
night before

Going to parties
and
Drinking up

Empty homes
and
Empty minds
Motherless
and
Fatherless

Family holding
no
meaning

Recollection of memories

making
childhood become haunting

Misunderstood
and
Unwanted
People find their feelings
As
nothing much

Life has become rather
Unvalued
As the highest goals held are
hopes of seeing tomorrow

Slowly the World
starts
to come to an end

And is surrounded
by
Darkness.

"A Life Long ago lived"

Some days it would just rain
But others her memories were left with stains.
That little girl she used to be-
Wasn't who she appeared to be,
She spent her days hiding her face-
In the days when at first she was only eight.
"Why does he hit you?"-
Her best friend would ask-
"He was upset, his day was bad",
"You can't let him keep hurting you- you have to call the cops",
"I can't, I won't, I'll never see my brothers or sisters again".
Day after day the friend tried to tell her-
Day after day the girl would lie-
The teachers would ask-
But she would never tell them-
She didn't how bad she was hurt-
As long as the others were safe & they all stayed together.
She promised them she'd get them out-
She promised one day they wouldn't have to live in fear-
She couldn't do much but say what she hoped would come true one day.
Then they moved when the girl was eleven-
One month from twelve-
But a few months later it started again-
The only difference was the abuser was a different man-
Just another new boyfriend that her mom thought was 'just perfect'.
This man and this girl got into a fight-
They threw words-

They threw punches-
But that was alright-
It must have been-
Because then her mother stood up & slapped her-
"You'll respect him, he's part of me"-
Her mother said.
Two days later the girl ran away to somewhere safe-
And turned in her mother & her mother's boyfriend.
Her and her siblings were taken away-
Separated for over a year,
But one day they joined together-
Only missing one.

Struggling

We all find ourselves knocking on closed doors,
Waiting for an opening to answers,
We all struggle with different things,
But really it's all the same,
We want to know why life seems so unfair,
We have all been left behind at some point in time in our lives,
We have all cried ourselves to sleep,
Wondering why we feel forgotten-unwanted-and unloved,
We wonder why our parents left us-without saying goodbye,
And it makes us wonder- did they ever truly love us,
We wonder what they would say if we confronted them,
We wonder why they didn't want us in their lives,
Then we find a place where we can hide-
And we breakdown and start to cry,
We try to forget the hurt we lock inside-
But it comes rushing out uncontrollable,
And I can't hide it anymore,
I'm hurting on the inside-
I heard she's taking care of someone else's kids-
She's loving them-
Why didn't she love me?
Why doesn't she care about me?
Why didn't she fight harder to try to keep me?
Why did she give up on me?
It seems like she has forgotten me,
And I cry myself to sleep at night,
I struggle to smile,

I struggle to remember that god loves me-
Because I feel unlovable,
I sat in church and every time they sing about love-
I cry-
I cry in the silence-
I cry in the crowd-
I cry all alone,
And I want to know how-
She couldn't take care of me?
She couldn't love me?
She won't call me?
Or call and ask of me, about me?
And I pray-
I pray for reassurance of god's love every day,
I pray for him to heal me.
And I know,
Even when I feel alone-unwanted-forgotten-unloved,
god's with me-
god wants me-
god hasn't forgotten me-
god loves me,
And he reassures me every day.
But the healing isn't over yet,
The healing has just begun,
So will you stay with me and help me through everything,
You're my family-
I feel safe with you-
And I need you now-
Because I'm struggling.

What you see & What you don't know

I'm not alright-
I act like I am-
I want to be-
Look at me (nothing's wrong)-
(Or so I try to make you believe)-
There's storms raging (on the inside)-
I feel (pain)-
(I want it to go away)-
And I don't want to (say anything)-
(not to anyone)-
I think-
(Maybe you'll see)-
(I want to scream)-
But I can't-
I don't (trust)-
(Not easily)-
I (only completely) trust (one person with) my feelings-
(She helps me)-
(Keeps me safe)-
(Keeps me from ending my own life)-
(And right now)-
I'm not alright.

———-

I'm not alright-
I act like I am-
I want to be-

Look at me-
There's storms raging-
I feel-
And I don't want to-
I think-
But I can't-
I don't-
I trust my feelings-
I'm not alright.

Dropped in My Head

He's so small & oh so young-
Its been over a year since I last saw him-
I miss him so much-
But I try to forget-
I guess that's all I really want-
Is to forget-
Forget who he is-
So I don't have to remember-
Sometimes I do almost forget-
But then as always he gets dropped in my head-
And then the memories play,
A constant film-
He came home my brother-
I took care of him-
I changed his diapers-
Right now I feel like I'm dying-
Like I want to be dead-
Wanting to go back to bad habits & addictions-
But still I feel a sea of sorrow flooding through me-
And once more I feel alone-
I feel like this will never end-
And in the end the memories stay never fading-
Just staying,
I had forgot about him until this morning-
Then she showed me the video-
And there again he was dropped in my head.

Sets of Three

Dreams-Wishes-Prayers
they come true
-sometimes it just takes time-
Love-Laugh-Live
people say
-some find it hard-
but they learn to.
Family-Friends-Eachother
everyone has someone
-sometimes it just takes a while to find them-
but everyone has someone.
Past-Present-Future
we all have one
-some are short others long, some hard others easy-
but we all have one.
And all good things come in sets of three.

Within the Morning

I woke within the morning
With an aching body
Tears nearly falling
I stretched-
More Pain-
I tossed-
I turned-
No comfort-
Just a sore aching body.
My legs they ached as if I ran for days without end-
My arms they ached as if I had held up the sky my entire life-
My feet felt as if stones and pebbles had taken root under my skin.
I took a breath-
That didn't hurt-
And as I listened to the constant in and out of children breathing
I realized my heart I couldn't feel beating-
I lay awake staring blankly into nothingness-
I let my thoughts carry me away-
I begin to think of someone-
And as my eyes begin to shut
I place my hand on my chest-
Within I can feel an unsteady pace of a beating heart-
And to this I found sleep once more within the morning.

Then and Now

Sometimes I set back and remanence,
I think of things I never said,
I wonder why things went the way they did,
Sometimes I ask myself,
Who are you?
How did you get to where you are?
And I ask once more,
Why did that happen?
Why did they do that?
Why did I listen and believe the lies they told,
How could I not see?
The beauty within me,
Within every word I wrote,
Within every word I spoke,
Yes, I know it takes time to heal,
But how much longer will it be until these stains I can no longer feel?
And yes again,
I know everything happens for a reason,
But it would be easier if you could tell me,
Why it happened when it did,
Why it happened period,
I don't like to look back,
At my past,
I don't like remembering,
But I like who came out the fire with a long-life desire,
To be someone,
To do something,

To change the cards laid in front of me,
Life is never easy,
But it is what you make it,
And anything is possible,
I was broken then,
I am together now.

More Than a Flower

The winter rose-
She carries the weight of a thousand worries,
Will she lose her petals?
Will the rain and snow sting?
Will her time here be of any importance to anything?
Who is she- but a little flower in a garden?
Who is she- how can she make a difference?
How is she who she is?
How is she what she is?
Why is it she blossoms better in darkness?
Why is it she prefers to become the sun?
Can this little flower bring hope to those who need it?
Can this little flower make it through the blizzards?
When will she see what everyone sees?
When will she see the beauty others claim to see?
When will she stop doubting?
Does the flower know there's more to life than broken dreams?
Does the little flower realize she can be more than a flower?
Does she know she's a flower because they say she is?
Does she know she doesn't have to be a flower-
she can be anything?
Where will she be when she blossoms?
But the most important question for her-
Where will she go at winter's end if she's only winter's rose?

Finding Ourselves

As the heavens ring out
The rains hurling down
Bring along the memories that struggle to resurface,
As the rage crashes onto the stones
The emotions inside scream for relief-
Scream to be let free
But I do not know how to release-
How to let this sorrow flee-
How to let go- and – just be me,
I do not know who I am
But I know each and every memory-
By heart,
I remember everything-
Just like it had happened-
Within these last second,
I remember who they are-
I remember who you are-
But I do not remember who I am,
I remember that life-
I know your life-
I know what's happening in this life-
I know my life-
But I wish I did not remember that life,
Other people do not make you who you are-
The scars that mark your heart-
The memories-
The fears-

Embedded in your mind and soul-
Make you who you are,
My memories-
My fears-
My scars-
Make me who I am,
My past does not determine who I am-
My past did not weaken me-
My past made me stronger,
And by choosing how my past will affect me-
I have chosen my path,
Our lives do not wait for us to catch up-
Just as our paths do not choose us-
We choose our paths,
We have the choice to change-
Change who we are,

We don't have to be who everyone tells us we are-
Or who everyone else wants us to be-
Only we know who we are-
But we have to look deep within to find ourselves-
We have to look past our pasts-
To find who we are-
And what we are capable of-
We are all special-
There is no such thing as ordinary-
Because everyone is extraordinary,
There are no two creatures-
No two beings in the world-
Who are the same in every way,
Everyone has been through different things-
Everyone has seen different things-
Everyone has seen tragedy-
Everyone has seen beauty,

But remember to always remember who you are-
Never forget the person you are on the inside-
The person you have always been-
And most importantly remember-
Do not lose yourself-
Don't let the world turn you into something or someone you're not,
Be yourself-
And if people don't love you for you then they're not worth your time,
Life is a gift-
Don't let it go to waste-
Don't let it pass you by-
And never forget who you are-
What you've lived through-
How special you are,
There is always someone out there who cares about you-
And no matter what there is always someone out there who loves you,
So, remember everything-
Forget nothing-
And know no matter how hard it seems sometimes you will make it through
the tough times-
Just to shine even brighter,
Remember you are the light in our darkened world,
Remember when you find yourself-
Be yourself-
Never try to be anyone else-
Never settle for anything less than being yourself,

Because you're one of a kind-
The one and only you-
You're an original,
And I guaranty there is no one like you-
Because you are the only you-
You are genuine-
Completely original,

So be who you are-
And I'll be who I am,
Always remember-
Never forget,
Forgive the ones who wrong you-
Love the ones who love you,
Love-
Never hate,
Befriend all-
Never shun people,
Remember-
And don't you ever forget.

The People in Your Life

In every dark moment there's always a light that shines through.
Those who bring light to your life-
Are meant to be in your life,
Those who bring darkness and chaos-
Are here for a moment to teach a lesson,
But what that lesson is you have to figure out for yourself.

A Friend I Have

When life wasn't my friend she was-
When I wanted death to be my end
She cried and held my hands-
She has shared in my sorrows
and I have shared in hers.
When nights began haunting us
We stood by each other and walked through the valley.
My life-
Her life-
Was as if death-
But we have shared in all joys as well.
When she smiles I smile.
When she laughs I laugh.
We're there for one another through the sunshine and rain.
Our friendship was destined-
Destiny I say.

"A Friend"

All I wanted was a friend,
During trials and tribulations.
Someone to hold my hand,
During suffering and separation.
Someone who would understand,
And be there to hold my hand.
To let me know,
Everything will be alright.
Someone to pick me up,
When I fall.
Someone to hold my hand,
And let me know,
That I'm Not Alone.

Seconds

Some days I count by seconds,
Sometimes I wish days flew like seconds,
Some seconds feel as if a life time,
Yet every second something changes,
-Love grows deeper-
-Faith grows stronger-
-Patience grows inevitably-
Life is measured by moments-
And moments in which accumulates over seconds,
It's the shortest seconds of my life that add up to be the most meaningful
moments,
So here I am counting the seconds,
Which for now just drag by,
But there I had stood trying to catch the seconds flying by,
Love- Faith- Patience- All & All,
Are growing remarkably,
And here & now I look back to the moments that mean the most,
And I realize they're caught in fleeting seconds.

There Had To Be A Last Day

There had to be a last day
My Dad and I sat together
I on the floor, he on the couch

As he brushed my hair for our 3rd grade piano recital.
There had to be a last day
When I would hear "I love you" from my dad
When he would teach me how to draw
Before his rights to me he signed away.
There had to be a last day
My Mom and I would play
I in her lap, we both on the floor
As the tickle monster took all my tickles away.
There had to be a last day
I felt loved by my parents
When it would've hurt to say goodbye
Before I looked forward to that last hour.
There had to be a last day
The meds and I claimed to be best friends
When the shrink finally said "you don't need antidepressants to stay okay"
All the while because I knew how to fake the perfect smile.
There had to be a last day
My heart and happiness would not be found where I had to stay
Leaving me with the pain of hurtful words
And making loving certain people seem absurd.
There had to be a last day
I took my last steps out unloving doors
Found a way out of living my worst horrors

No more pain, no more sorrow, now I'm looking forward to a better happier tomorrow.

Family

Family is not defined-
By anything-
The blood running through our veins-
Those we're born from-
Those we're raised by-
Our DNA.
Family is not-
Based on-
Similar appearances-
Hair-
Eyes-
Lips-
Noses-
Height-
Intelligence-
(Academic- or- Street).
Family is-
Acceptance-
Encouragement-
Guidance-
Relentless Love-
Never-ending Hope-
Family-
Never stops-
Trying-
Reaching out-
Pulling each other up-

Caring-
Family-
Loves to no relent.

My Nana

Gentle soothing hands
Warm embracing arms
Soft and comforting voice
A welcome smile
An open heart
An ear always waiting to hear
Cradling
Rocking
Reading to
A first home
A forever home
In her heart and in her arms
First lesson of love
First lesson of the meaning of love
Watching her teaches how to love
A very special person
Someone I'll always hold near to my heart
My Great-Grandma
My Nana.

A Poem is

A structured passage
That speaks to the heart
And
Comes from life experiences
From confusion
From attempts to piece together
Or
To thank
To rejoice
To express feelings.
A structured passage
That's never structured the same way twice
And
Is different depending on the author
The artist
The poet.
A completely unstructured structured passage
That can consist of:
Similes -like or as-
Metaphors -that are-
Hyperboles -bigger than the universe-
Idioms.
Or at least that's what one is to me...
Sometimes...

I'm sorry

I'm sorry,
I'm sorry I couldn't save you from her,
I'm sorry I couldn't save you from him,
I'm sorry I wasn't always there,
I'm sorry I wasn't there to protect you,
I'm sorry for waiting two years before telling anyone what was done to us,
I'm sorry for acting like I don't love y'all,
I'm sorry for never wanting to talk to y'all about our bio-parents,
I'm sorry for letting all those people hurt you,
I'm sorry for leaving y'all alone and defenseless,
I'm sorry for letting y'all live in fear for so long,
I'm sorry for not being the best sister I could have been,
I'm so so so very sorry for everything,
Will y'all please forgive me?

Bitter Sweet

I spend my days waiting for dawn,
Or at least an hour with shade,
The shadows I once knew,
The shadows I grew up with have now inhabited my living space-
Where my heart hides the secrets of who I really am.
Waiting for my next rush-
No matter the pain it causes-
In constant denial of what it does to me.
The high is bitter sweet-
Knowing the next will never be as good as the one before-
But for now it suffices.
And now the sharpness & weight of bricks that run through me-
With every breath & every sound-
Beg me to stop-
But the rest of me longs for more.
The more I have-
The sweeter my sleep-
Never have I rested with such peace.
Maybe just one more-
Can I have one more night with this peaceful sleep I may never hold again-
If I give up this bitter sweet rush.

"Not a Girl"

Being a female doesn't make me a girl-
I'm not afraid of dirt-
I can lift heavy stuff-
And if I break a nail or my hair gets ripped out-
Oh well- who cares?!-
They'll grow back.
You can open the door
Because that's polite
You can say "Yes ma'am"
Because I say "Yes sir"
But don't treat me as if I'm a little girl-
Afraid of dirt-
Afraid to scuff up my shoes-
To break my nails-
To lose some hair-
Afraid to mess up new clothes,
Because I'm not.
So don't treat me like a girl-
Just because I'm a female.

"I'm Not Angry"

I've been told-
"Get mad! Be mad! Show them you're angry!"
But I can't be angry-
Angry hurts-
Angry sends sharp pains stabbing through my heart
&
Then through the rest of me.
I've been told to shout & yell-
But I can't-
No sound comes out-
Plus, I don't like loud-
Can I just stay quiet?
Quiet in my own space?
I don't yell or shout whether it's good or bad.
Yet I'm told to be angry-
To get angry-
But that's not who I AM is-
So that's not who I'm going to be.
You can tell me BE ANGRY!-
But I won't do it!
I will raise my voice & act upset-
If only that will keep you from getting mad-
But as soon as you leave or turn your back-
I'll apologize for what I said or did,
Because I love Love-
I hate Hurt-
And I refuse to be someone's source of pain-

I won't hurt anyone-
I REFUSE TO BE SOMEONE ELSE'S PAIN!
I'm sorry-
Wait! No I'm not,
Because this is me-
Who I am-
And I will not be like you.
I still care-
I still Love You-
But my way-
Not yours.

Dream not Disclosed

Hello dear friend,
Only one dream I can remember-
But I wish not to disclose the details-
For this dream as I had seen-
Was quiet disturbing-
And in all actuality could have been real.
So for the sake of your time-
And the comfortability that has become mine,
I will not disclose what was my dream.
Though ask-
I will give no answer,
Though you may pry to figure it out,
I fear this dream was nearly an actual event-
Being spun by my mind's hands of time.
So if you will dear friend-
Accept my answer,
And be on your way-
I'd very much be obliged.
For now until next,
Old friend I beg to you to say goodbye.

A More Welcoming Place

In the distance-
The creaking branches roar.
In solemn places-
The water runs dry as an attempt to escape human lips.
What places have I yet to go that have not beckoned me to stay?
What places shall I roam never see?
Where trees dance beneath scowls of a heartless moon-
Where daisies cry because the sun b'eth harsh.
No place I've gone-
Where valleys don't mourn,
No place I've seen-
Where the mountains do not shake or crumble.
A scarlet sea of distress beckons me to stay and help the people escape to-
A more welcoming place.

To Have A Power

If I had a power-
I would hope for the power to heal.
To save a life from pain,
To remove lost hope-
If a power is what I had-
I would hope it be that to heal.

Powerful

In the distance the creaking branches roar.
In solemn places the places the water runs dry as an attempt to
escape these human lips.
What places have I yet to go that have not beckoned me to stay.
What places shall I roam but never see?
Where trees dance beneath the scowls of heartless moon.
Where daises cry because the sun b'eth harsh.
No place I've gone where valleys don't mourn,
No place I've seen where the mountains do not shake or crumble.
A scarlet sea of distress beckons me to stay and help the people
escape to more welcoming place.

Treehouse

Deep in the woods
What a mystical land!
A tree stands tall and in its hands-
It cradles a home of magnificent stories and tales-
From times and lands of long ago.
Beneath the leaves you would expect death and decay-
But instead in life of creatures never known to the men of today.
This treehouse grows up-
Outstretched towards the sky-
While inspiration is birthed inside.

Prompted with Ice

Ice storms reveal the ice-covered hearts within empty chests-
The brokenness beneath the porcelain masks-
Families that would be best with one person less-
The problems that probe right under the surface and beckon to us-
Warm hearts thaw the ice- maybe that's why the world is still frozen-
because warm hearts are rare-
At least in this realm-
We or better I learned that the darkness lurks at bay and beckons to be
welcomed to stay-
Spirituality sensitive my emotions turn to inner chaos and my spirit yearns
to be free somewhere where the darkness isn't so thick and heavy,
The ice is a jail cell with a frozen interior-
The bars nothing more than bitter and cold hearts-
What's a family when there's more anger than love?
Why exert yourself when no one shows appreciation or gratitude?
How do you stay okay when you feel like people are never satisfied, like
what you do is never good enough?
No matter how hard you try, no matter how much you help, they focus on
everything that's wrong with you?
I used to feel loved,
But it's not like it used to be,
I feel love here and there every once in a while,
But here lately I just feel like feeling loved is something of the past,
We have good days but it seems like there are more bad days than good-
I don't understand why there's always something wrong with me or
something wrong with the way I am,
It's just something I don't understand-

These are the things I learned when the ice rained down and decided it
wanted to stay and watch us humans play-
We had a few good days-
We played spades and poker.
But there was yelling and anger throughout these last few cold and bone
chilling days-
In those days I prayed for night to come soon arrive so I could escape to
place where only god and I would exist-
I prayed and I talked to god-
god and I carried on many conversations and I know the ice resting in hearts
will melt with time-
And I know I'll be alright as long as god is by my side-
As long as I can hear god's voice-
As long as god and I can find a place of quietness where only WE exist-
That's what I learned, explanation and all while attempting to make the best
of a frozen situation.

Shallow Hollow Grave

My chest feels like a shallow grave
I know it won't be long until they come to hallow it out.
My heart beats at an unconscious pace The bell will ring when there's a
melody When it does, they'll hollow out this grave
Leaving behind an empty tomb Healing all these open wounds
This day is soon But not today
And here I wake to a new tune
The pounding of shovels against the dirt takes my mind off the loss of air,
still encased in a shallow grave
With it slowly being hollowed out I know a melody, a tune will beat
But for now...
My chest remains a shallow grave.

She is Beautiful

Death will find you some day.
And when she does-
You will love her-
For everything she is.
Death is beautiful in every way-
No matter how she shows herself-
You will love her for who she is.
Death isn't about the time or place-
'Cause she is beautiful in everyway.
Death isn't about the who or how-
She is simply a way out.
Death is beautiful, unless you take your life yourself.
She is freedom-
She is an escape-
Death is unique in every way.
I wouldn't be able to live in this place-
Without knowing she will find me someday-
And it will be my time to say goodbye.

Words

More than letters More than sounds
They're a swinging door Into the heart
Into the mind They paint pictures Blacks- Whites- Greys And vivid colors
They're wrote on paper They come from the heart They're shared by mouth
We hear them We see them We share them We say them
We think them We hold them We hid them

We take them They're there in lead They're there in ink
But yet,
The most meaningful are there- are here-
In breath.

Writer's Block

If you write please tell me this,
Have you ever felt trapped?
Like you're at a loss of words?
Nothing, everything gone?
You feel so much emotion,
But yet you have no words,
Like there's no way to get it out?
You feel trapped inside yourself,
And the walls around you are blank,
Everything you look at seems to be closing in,
Like you're blocked-
Blocked from life itself?
This happens to me frequently,
I call it writer's block.
It's when your emotions are on overdrive-
Life feels like it's spinning-
You have so much to say-
So much you could write about-
But you have no words.
No words to speak-
No words to sing-
NO WORDS TO WRITE.
This is my writer's block.

The Block

It's like when you're drawing,
And your paper has nothing but faded lines-
From erasing and erasing and erasing,
Make you-
Make me-
Feel trapped 'cause there's a world full of words but yet I can't find the right
ones.

The Grey Space

This space between me and life is dark grey- Bleak and cold
Haunting and cruel
The space begs to be filled
-not with love or wealth
-but with things that cause one to slowly die The high, the grey, beckons to
return
With eyes opened With eyes shut
All I see is a dark bleak grey space empty, all but me
-No words
-No want to feel
-No want for emotions
-No need to release, only to escape the bleakness taking hold inside.
All grey every second-
Slow and torturous, the moments my body forces me to breathe
My body cries to inhale but I cry for my next breath not to reach my lungs-
-whether I go to heaven or hell

-whether there really is a heaven or hell Only the demons surrounding me
Only the monsters inside of me
Really know the truth of what waits after I escape into the bleak dark grey.

Grey

What beauty the sky holds when grey- When gently lilacs they lay-
Sweet nothings are whispers, so they say- As the sky's painter paints it grey.
So softly these flowers lay- In whites, purples, and greys-
As hushed voices tremble and pray-
For those lost to the color grey.
In distant lands from far away-
Where those are seen floating with glowing flames of grey- The lost are set
out on the water's bay-
With hopes of vibrant color replacing the grey. In time it is said night will
turn to day-
But for now, time is embraced in a growing grey- It's this same wish to slay-
To never lose another to grey.
Yet the painter may- Paint the sky daily grey-

So not to forget the light of each sun ray-
For only the painter can both paint and take away what is done by the color
grey.

Purple

Purple
purple are the tears cried
in sorrow for what is known
because of wisdom of things foretold.
Purple is the color clinging at souls filled with power from a source
commonly
seen as unknown.
Purple covers the fears within
by a saving grace that lives within
Purple is the strongest of friends for all that it represents.
Purple comes in many colors lilac, violet, fuchsia, and more it comes in
many shades
seen as pastel, neon, and more.
Purple stands for extraordinary things.
Purple is seen as royalty known with wisdom felt with spirituality
Purple provides power over obstacles it transforms
and it gives a sense of nobility.
Purple- purple is both seen and unseen.

Pink Petals Fall

As pink petals fall to earth the earth is covered
yet awakened.
One petal
Two petals
Three petals
Four
Open your eyes
Start on your chores.
Five petals
Six petals
Seven petals
Eight
Don't fret
True love is never late.
Eight petals
Seven petals
Six petals
Five
True friendship is like a honey love hive.
Four petals
Three petals
Two petals
One
Spiritual awakening for those searching passes none.
Pink petals they fall
Each with a single gift.
One petal- true love

Two petals- friendship
Three petals- attraction
Four petals- more
Five petals- romance
Six petals- spiritual awakening
Seven petals- togetherness
Eight petals- more
Each petal falls gifting the world providing a new story for all.
One
Two
Three
Four
Five
Six
Seven
Eight Petal
Awakened and covered all at once the earth lays beneath a blanket of petals.
And still Pink Petals Fall.

White

Cleansing- Purifying- Gratifying
White.
Washing over the world
Coating the ground in sticky powder
Small glitters of light.
A smile dancing across a face
A twinkle
A gleam in starry eyes.
Bright shining stars in a night sky
Light- light- oh so very bright.
Walls
Blinds
Curtains
Hospitals
Schools
Churches
They all are painted
All decorated
In a :
Pure
Clean
Holy
Color
So simple
So bright
So clean and pure
The color coating the world

in
White.

154

Snow

A barrier blankets the ground
As angels softly shed loose feathers
As their wings expand
So as does the covering over the land-
This reflector of light blinds the dark
Yet blankets the sky
As where there is no longer color.
I shift in my seat and glance out the window
And wonder how birds fly in such weather.
As if a blizzard small white feathers glide throughout the sky
Only to realize they're not feathers
But softly frozen tears from heaven.
The world is cold and cruel
So, the tears of angels above freeze as they enter the atmosphere.

And now create a blanketing barrier of cold ice and unfriendly frozen tears.

On The Wings of Cupid

The ticking hands of time
Slowly consuming my life
Rip apart the dreams I'm dreaming and devour me from the inside
Though it seems dark
All I see is light
In a world full of chaos
I hang onto the tips of Cupid's wings as he carries me to love
A shore so far away
Yet I'm standing in its waves
As the sea stings my open wounds
I find the sweet torture a bliss moment in remembrance
Of whom I was and now who I am and no longer am I the same
For time takes small pieces of life and forever changes the inside
With this I see plans unseen
And feel the torturous beauty of silent prayers and patience

And somehow,
I know this love will withstand and consume this life
But, until it does,
I'll let Cupid carry me to a distant shore where time consumes but never
steals the life which is brought from lightness of heart and mind.

Bandage

Hearts were meant to be held-
Hearts were meant to be healed-
Gently holding hands cradling fragile hearts-
Their job to shield-
Some pain enters-
That's the way the Creator intended-
But if we hold onto each other's hearts-
Bandages wont be needed-
Because our love for one another will heal the heart faster than band aids
and antibiotics-
No pain killers will be needed-
As long as we have each other-
My heart was made for you-

So, I place it in your hands-
And here in your hands-
I feel open wounds slowly closing-
I realize the healing-
It comes with true love's holding of the heart-
Hearts were meant to be held-
So, if you want, please hold mine-
Hearts were meant to be healed-
So, if you would continue to cradle my heart as it heals-
And if your heart feels the same-
I promise to take extra special care-
For I want to be your heart's only bandage.

A Silent Face

Nothing out from between my lips-
They're sealed...
It's your turn to tell me what you see,
How do you feel?
Do you see me the way I see you?
Do you love me the way I love you?
No matter what you say or do I will Forever and Always love you,
No matter what.
Do you still love me?
Do you still feel the same?
Has anything changed?
My heart belongs to you and always will,
No one else will it ever belong to but you...
I will love you, even after the end appears to have come...

My heart is in your hands
Take my heart and never give it back,
Because its only fully whole in your hands and it belongs with you,
So, keep it Forever and Always with you in your hands...
I want to scream my love for you from rooftops...
Please be mine,
so I can be yours because I'm already yours,
I just want everyone to know...
I want to spend the rest of my life waking up telling you how much you
mean to me...
It's you I dream of,
It's you my heart beats for,

It's you I love...
I want to share the rest of my
- the rest of my time-
with you...
You're everything I'll ever need...

I learned how to love when I met you...
I will never love another the way I love you...
I wish I knew just how you truly feel about me...
I want to stay wrapped in your arms Forever and Always...
The way these feelings only grew stronger...
These feelings never fade...
The words come when I'm with you...
Heart, Mind, and Spirit...
I've always loved you...
These feelings never fade.

Never Wrong- if – It's Alright

Love to some is a simple word,
Love to some is a feeling,
To some a simple explanation,
To others an array of colors,
Some base love on a feeling,
On a sense of comfort,
On a look-
a touch-
the sound of someone's voice.
But this isn't love.
Love-
Love is a constant reminder of what makes you whole-
Love is a constant reminder of what makes you complete-
What you can't live without-
Or better yet,
who you can't live without-
Love is knowing no matter where you are or were you're going when you get
back its going to be waiting there for you.
Love is trusting without question-
Love is open never hiding anything-

Love is knowing when something goes wrong you have arms to run to-
Love is more than a word,
because its more than words can explain-
Love is more than a feeling,
because it's still there even when you become emotionally numb-
Love is more than on explanation,

because it can't be defined by books-
Love is more than an array of colors,
because colors come nowhere close to expressing the greatness of it-
And yet to each individual
Love is something different never the same-
but never wrong-
as long as it's alright.

When I Miss Like This

Tears drown my heart-
Not necessarily sad-
Not necessarily bad-
These tears try to escape my eyes-
But instead, they come out of my mouth-
And onto paper-
With you seeming so far-
Yet so close-
My heart leaps to you to see-
And to you to see when I think-
I smile-
But to you to not see when I think-
I hold in-
I hold back tears-
To not have you here with me-
For you not to be right by my side-
To know I want to see you in time-
And for me all I do is pray-
And wish-
For what seems a long time-
Will fly by and show itself to be short.
And in feeling this-
And in knowing this-
All that's left to come out
Are the words:
"I miss you, when I miss like this".

Warmth

My hair falls shielding my face-
Covering the shallow smile that barely peeks over my lips-
As water begins to seep into and cover my eyes-
The sun's rays break through the ice-cold barrier surrounding the world
around me-
And it begins to thaw me and warm the ice inside-
This warmth consumes me-
This warmth takes hold of my heart and makes it impossible for me to not
care-
(Not to love- Not to comfort- To hurt-
To shun-
To never give a second chance- Never to forgive)-
This warmth makes it all impossible-

Warmth doesn't come through the blinding rays of light-
Warmth I learned comes through love.
After learning-
After experiencing-
Warmth-
Still my hair falls shielding my face-
Yet it no longer covers a shallow smile-
Or-
Crying eyes-
It draws attention to-
Smiling eyes-
And
A genuine smile.

My hair falls shielding my face-
Yet I glow to bright to be covered or hidden.

So Often

So often I'm told "You're kill'n the mood"
So often I reply "I know, it's my specialty"
But I find it funny:
Because it's not ever "a mood"
Because it's simply a simple expression of feelings.
So often I wonder how love can feel the same yet different:
To love, it feels one way
To love, it feels another way.
So often I wonder how feelings differ between individuals
How love feels this way with one
How love feels that way with another.
No, these things don't bother me
These things are things I simply wonder and ponder upon.
"A mood"
"Love itself"
"A feeling"
"It's ironic"
"It's somehow funny"
-the way this all makes me feel-
So often.

How Love is Meant to be

The tears we cry for those we've lost
The smiles we share with those we love
The laughter that rings all around
Remembering those moments
Remembering all good memories
Holding tight to all that's good
Holding hands and pulling close
Holding hearts close to ours
Taking even more careful steps
Taking notice of each person
This is love how it's meant to be
Love:
Hurts with one another
Gives hope to one another
Mourns with one another
Love:
Smiles-
Laughs-
and Cries together
Love:
Lives-
Grows-
and Breathes together
Love:
Holds-
Binds-
and keeps together

When here
Or
Even gone
Love will for always live on.

Two Hearts

How two hearts grow so close-
Even in the midst of distance-
I know not,
nor do I understand,
But the feeling I share...
It becomes as if the two hearts merge into one.

I Miss You

It's like the rushing of water
The quaking of the earth
It is the aching within my chest
The trickling tears cascading down my cheeks
It comes
But never leaves
With every breath
Every dream
It grows every second,
minute,
hour
It grows more and more,
day by day
This...
This me missing you.

The more I miss you
The more I Love You
Its unescapable:
I cry
I laugh
I smile
I dream
With every:
tear
laugh
smile

night...
I think of You.
And I Miss You.

Missing You Is

Missing you is like missing the Sun
It's like a decade of constant rain No warmth
Just cold bursts of wind that chills to the core.
Missing You is like being trapped under water
It's like having no air in the atmosphere
A weight heavy chest
Sinking my lungs filling with the ocean's seas.
Missing You is like the falling of Autumn's leaves
It's like the darkening of all the colors
A blanket of snow and ice
Causing a desolate void of distance
Missing You is like holding a crushed heart
It's like looking inside to realize you're empty
A puzzle piece unable to be found
Only able to complete a complete picture with You.
Missing You is like a stop in time
It's like the earth has stopped spinning
And where once there was floating
We've,
I've, been smacked to the cold hard ground.
Missing You is Me Missing a part of Myself.

Still

<u>*(To Be Treated Right for the First Time)*</u>

I can still feel:
Your lips pressed against my lips,
Your hands on my hips,
Your fingers running through my hair.
I remember:
You picking me up and carrying me up a hill,
You spinning me around like a princess,
Your hand in my hand.
I can still hear:
You whispering in my ear,
You singing for me every time we talked,
You saying "I'm so glad we're finally together".
I can still:
Feel your arms wrapped around me,
See your face right in front of me,
Hear your voice saying the sweetest of things to me.
And
I still:
Miss everything about you.
I still:
Want to be with you.

A Mother's Love

173

Our Marieah

Just one day here and there
This is what I want
Everyday here with us
This is all I wish
To do her hair
To put it up or to braid it in tiny braids
This is what I want
To hold her
To rock her to sleep and kiss her goodnight each night
This is all I wish
To hear her voice
To hear her laugh and see her smile
This is what I want
To watch her grow up
To see her be the best big sister
This is all I wish
To comfort her when she cries
To let her know everything will be alright that we're right here with her
This is what I want
To have her in my arms
To have all these moments with her
This is all I wish
To call her name and her answer from the other room
To call her name outside and hear her come running inside for dinner
This is what I want
For a piece of my heart to not be so far away
But instead only a breath away

This is all I wish
To take her back and forth from school
To help her get ready for prom
To see what she thinks is stylish
To hear her favorite song
Or to even know if she'd have a favorite song and if so what it would be
This is what I want
To have been able to carry her for 9 whole months in my womb
To be able to carry her in my arms now not just in my heart
This is all I wish
To have each moment
To be able to watch her sleep
To hear her breathe
To see her play
To know her voice
To learn her favorite color
To learn her favorite food
To know everything about her
To hold tight and close
This is what I want
To have our Marieah back
This is all I wish.

Bearable

I'm still breathing
I know the rain will stop
I know the pain can't last forever
My heart's still beating
I know the tears I've cried weren't in vain I know the prayers I pray are
heard
Though it hurts
I know it won't hurt forever
Though I cry
I know I won't cry forever
This pain I feel
These tears I cry
This sense of hopelessness inside
It makes it hard to stand But I do it anyways
I can't sleep
But when I do, I can't escape my dreams
I want to cry
Without end
Yet I know None of These will last forever
And in knowing this
It makes it all...
Bearable.

Questions Wondered of a Child Lost

Some have said "at least your have the twins"
And to them I say I am grateful for the children I have that live-
that breathe.
But one child cannot be replaced by the existence of another-
Each hold a different place in the heart.
And where my daughter would be has for 6 years been the place within
where a gaping space has hollowed through.
The questions that will forever be unanswered:
Who would she be?
How would she communicate with me?
What would all her favorites be?
Would she look like her brothers?
(Everyone says they had the same nose)
Would the doctors have been right?
Would I have learned brail and sign language just so she could speak with
me?
What would life be like with her living-
With her breathing breaths with me, with her brothers?
What would live entail if she was here with me?

As I Cry Myself to Sleep

Sometimes I set back and ask-
Am I really a good mother?
There's times when I don't even know myself-
And I wonder am I damaging the ones I love the most?
How can I give them a whole life when most of the time I don't feel whole
inside?
How do I heal the shattered pieces-
How do I show them I love them more than life?
Do they know they're the reason I survived - the hardest time of my life.
Do they know my heart only beats because of their existence-
If it wasn't for them I would have already let go of me.
But I fight to find someone I recognize-
Someone who is buried inside.
Not for me
Just for them
I want to give them the best of me even though I'm not always sure who
that is or where that part of me went.
I don't ever want to be my parents-
I want my kids to know that their always loved and safe at home.
I was covered in bruises-
My innocence was stolen-
I lived feeling like there was no way out
I thought, surely I'll die before I reach the age to decide anything of my own
life.
I thought the pain would never end until it erased me from my own
existence.
But somehow I'm here despite the emptiness,

Somehow I survived a broken life.
Now I'm trying to find the parts me I hid away,
Trying to learn how to be my own saving Grace.
Because that weight isn't meant to be carried by them,
I need to learn how to live for myself.
My life shouldn't be their burden to bare.
And here I am breaking down in tears as they dream,
Every night as they sleep I close my eyes and feel the sting
As tears burn through my skin.
I wonder why I was the post everyone leaned on when I was just a little kid?
I won't make my kids bare that weight,
They will get the childhood that wasn't in my fate.
They won't have to worry about fists flying at them or someone who
shouldn't be in their bed.
They won't know the pain I felt growing up how I did.
They won't have their innocence stripped from them.
They'll know love,
They'll know life is worth living,
They'll know they'll never be alone.
And though I fight to keep my memories away so I don't break down in
front of their faces,
I still cry because I feel somehow I'm always failing them.
What does it mean to be a good parent to them?
The mirror my inner self looks at is shattered- it's full of cracks,
So it's hard to see which reflection belongs to the me I'm searching for.
Parenting while healing from trauma is hard.

The Eyebrow Song

(in the tune of "You are sixteen going on seventeen")

You have eyebrows 1,2 eyebrows
And they're starting to show
They're starting to match the hair on your head
And you're looking so cute

For the Boys

I loved you yesterday and every day before your birth
I love you today and I will love you tomorrow and every day thereafter
My love for you grows more and more each day
You're my love
You're my heart
You're my every breath
I love you with all my heart
With all my soul
I love you with the very essence of my being
You're my love
You're my life
I love you to no end

I loved you yesterday and every day before your birth
I love you today and I will love you tomorrow and everyday thereafter.

You Are

<u>*(a song for my children)*</u>
You are the rain that nourishes my soul-
You are everything I could dream of-
And so much more-
You are the warmth of my soul-
Even when the sun does not show-
I breathe for you-
I fight for you-
I live because of you-
When your spirit chose to live with mine-
I knew I would always love you-
Through hard times-
Through dark times-
Even when my health declines-
I breathe for you-
I fight for you-
I live to stand by you-
I will always accept you just as you are-
I will support you and guide you no matter where you are-
Because I love you unconditionally-
You are the reason my heart still beats-
My miracles-
My gifts from the stars-
You don't just hold a special place within my heart-
You are the special place from where my love starts-
My rainbow-
My children-

My precious gifts-
The gods knew with you I would choose to live-
Through the hard times-
Through the dark times-
Even when my health declines-
I will always fight to remain by your side-
You are the rain that nourishes my soul-
You are the warmth of my soul-
Even when the sun does not show-
You are the special place from where my love begins-
You are everything I could dream of-
And so much more-
Thank you for being my reason to live each day-
Even when the world turns you away-
To me you can always run-
My love for you will forever carry on-
I breathe for you-
I fight for you-
I live because of You.

Union's Heart

184

this love is strong

As sure as willows weep
As sure as the crow caws
As sure as water runs
I know this love is strong.

My Love to You

I want to be the gentlest of love to ever touch your heart
The softest and safest love you've ever felt
I want my love to be the love that keeps you warm
I want my love to be the love you've dreamed about
I want my love to be the love you always choose
To make you smile, laugh, and bring gleams into your eyes
To fill your heart with comfort, peace, security
This is what I want my love to be for you.
-Love You Endlessly & Eternally

The Universe in Her Eyes

As the sunlight hits your eyes swirls of ember and deep earth collide-
In moonlight your eyes glow with the light of every star-
Within them I watch the story of creation unfold,
Every secret within the universe is made known as our eyes meet locking the moment into memory.
My love for you will never fade it grows deeper and stronger each and every day.
And when we are apart it feels as if the universe has abandoned me ceasing to exist.
And when I'm met with your embrace I have no doubt that I am home and I am safe.
In a world where I experienced cruelty from an early age I've now learned how it feels to know unconditional love that cannot be erased,
You have taught me I'm able to be loved and me existing is reason enough.
And I love you no matter what.
You do not need to do- just be,
Be you as you have always been.
Because without you my lungs could not breathe another breath and my universe would cease to exist.

To Think Of Sweetness, To Think Of You

Your beauty exceeds the mundane
My love for you is not bound by the restraints of time, space, or this
reincarnation for I will find you in every life after this one
My spirit will search for you in every lifetime
My spirit longs to entwine with yours, never unentangling
I want to be by your side for the rest of this life and every life after this one
for all of eternity
You shine brighter than the rays of sunlight at the height of noon
You glow brighter than the beams of moonlight that cascades across an open
meadow under a new moon on a clear night

Your eyes twinkle brighter than the flickering of a million stars combusting
as space creates paintings beyond earth's atmosphere
Yet no creation, no painting made by the hand of a human, or painting
made by nature itself comes close to comparing to the delicate and exquisite
beauty in the details of every aspect of your being
From the sweet melody of your spoken words to the sound of soothing
waters your voice transmits as you sing
The joy that radiates from you as you dance normally to the stillness and
peace that envelopes the atmosphere when you slow dance
I stand,
I sit,
I watch and stare,
I dream,
I think,
All in awe of you,
My darling beautiful goddess I love and adore you

And I wish to spend every life with you
And to spend the rest of our lives adorning you with love and affection and
anything and everything I can.

189

More Than Love Can Explain

Your Earth Crystal eyes that shine in the light amber, chocolate, and earth melting into each other
I stare into those crystals and see where nature finds its home where the spirit of the earth finds comfort and rest
And when you smirk,
I see a look full of youthfulness-
Sweet yet mischievous as if you've danced with the fae
When you smile that heart filled smile,
I see the glistening of the sun reflecting off of a thousand waters
And when you laugh it fills the space with a sense of calmness and in this calmness,
I find joy
The very essence of your being brings me to my knees in awe and wonder of you

Your personality that breaks through the darkness of any day
Your comfort and love that envelops me when chaos and stress swells up inside of me
Your mellifluous voice that cascades upon my ears draws me in as if a bear to honey
Your touch radiates through me as if electrical currents are pulsating through me and bringing me back to life
Your kiss is soft and delicate, yet fierce and passionate
It brings the world to a halt for a fleeting moment
And my longing for you and my desire to see you and to be seen by you and only you swells up and intoxicates me,
Leaving me completely defenseless for that fleeting moment

I will spend the rest of time being mesmerized and awestruck by everything
about you,
From your personality to your perspective on things,
From your laugh to your voice when you speak or sing,
From your warm embrace to your soft fingertips gently trailing across my
skin,
From your earth crystal eyes to your small
dainty feet-
Every inch of you, every particle of your being,
Every last bit of your essence entrances me and draws my spirit nearer to
yours longing to not just be entranced
But to be entwined with you
My spirit longs to be entwined with you,
Not just physically
But mentally, emotionally, spiritually
My spirit longs to be entwined and entangled with you on both a particle
and quantum level,
Longing to merge wavelengths and to melt into each other as one.

Love's Secret Winter

My love for you is overwhelming
To feel forced to have to contain it is unbearable
Not being able to show you the physical affection I wish you would allow
me to fills my entire being with immense sorrow
I feel as if oceans of tears hide behind my eyes afraid to pour out
How do I explain this feeling I feel?
How is it possible to be overwhelmed by the weight of my love for you that
I'm not allowed to show?
Great sorrow and grief feel me at my core
Great agony sits on our bedside
What sorrows and pain my heart is burdened with
For true love is such beauty yet full of deep aches within the heart
This pain unfolds to longing- longing that seems unattainable
This in which my heart longs for and craves feels as if to remain a void
I know not how to overcome or simply how not to care
I know not how to speak these words though I am able to write them so
well
How do I say just what I feel?
How do I use my voice?
Why is it this longing never existed before I met you but somehow its now
unbearable?
It's as if the air is stuck within my chest
As if my heart skips many beats only halfway keeping me alive
I feel sharp pain deep within
I feel seas ebb near the surface
I love you immensely and though words of love seem to suffice for you-

They feel to me unable to fully convey the capacity to which I feel this love
for you
I hold within all this love which is bursting inside
The seams that loosely hold me together I fear are ripping apart within me
I wish to love you in every way to adorn you with affection:
To kiss
To hold
To feel you near
To be entangled passionately
I want to be for you all you are for me
To give to you in every way you give unto me
Our union has filled my spirit and heart with happiness to the brim
Yet as of late, this love I feel for you has brought to heart such pain
I feel deep sorrow
I feel deep pain
They fill my waking moments
They consume almost every thought
This sorrow and this pain make me question:
Am I really enough?
Is there something wrong with me?
Have I done something wrong?
Why do you not want me to embrace you or adorn you with a kiss?
Are you simply overstimulated or is it something more?
Is there a reason why I feel only I crave a closeness that we both used to
explore?
What beauty love douth portray whilst in the midst of a blooming spring
that's seen
Yet beyond one's sight love just as well exists within an icy winter that leaves
behind no life
A pain like loss
A pain almost as deep as death
This is the pain that I feel within as I learn of love's secret winter.

Pools of Earth

It's the mudded pools of earth that light shines upon-
They're what you only perceive to be your eyes,
But to I they're a story passed down over thousands of years as if your eyes
tell of every lifetime you've lived before this-
It's as if the voice of earth has painted the windows into your soul ever so
delicately-
Her words swirl in the wind and her spirit leaps from within to paint the
work of art that stands before me-
This work of art that both silences me in awe and excites me into
conversation-
This work of art that makes my heart skip a beat and my skin dance in pure
bliss-
Every precise detail that's been sculpted perfectly-

And as I gaze upon her work of art and her voice radiates around me,
I feel myself slowly falling into the earth herself-
I can't help but hope to be able to gaze upon the earth's work of art for all of
this lifetime.

Be Free With Me

Let yourself be free with me.
I hear the words you speak unto me,
You fear what you could do to me- if you let yourself be free.
If only you could see,
I'm not a delicate flower in need of shielding.
There is a difference between the pain of abuse and the pain of pleasure.
When will you hear my cries from within to let yourself be free with me?
Uncage the animal you lock inside,
Cast its restraints to the side,
Allow the animal within you to be free when it is just you and I.
I crave a pain only given by pleasure's hands.
Release the animal within,
Let it dig its fingertips into my skin.
Grip the bones at my hips,
Let it sink its teeth into my skin.
Let it mark me as its own.
I beg of you,
Do not fear the pain it could bring,
Do not worry about me.
Uncage the animal within you,
Let me feel the chains of its love wrap around me,
Its claws dig into me,
Let me feel the animal tear through my flesh then lick the wounds it gave
me,
Let me hear its deep growl escape your lungs,
Let me hear its howl release as it to finds pleasure in the pain it inflicts on
me.

Worry not of my physical wounds,
They heal faster than you think.
Worry not of creating fear,
I crave the pain given by the animal within you.
Do not deny yourself a single part of who you are,
Embrace every aspect of yourself and allow it to always be free when you are
with me.
I will keep you and your inner animal safe,
Just as you keep every part of me safe.
So,
I beg of you,
Free the animal within,
Fear not the pain that may come from its hands,
I crave your inner animal just I crave you
when calm and content.

An Age Unanticipated

It's Not Mean To Say No

I will say "No, please don't" the first time
But if it seems like you did not hear me-
Or you did not care-
Than it won't be as nice the next time my voice rings out through the air
I do not need to give a reason
My body is my own
Even if you don't like my decision you still need to leave me alone.

Here Together

In a world overran by those who don't care about anyone but their self
I'm here and I see you
I know you don't believe me yet but it's true
I'm here with you
I've seen you on your darkest days and I'm not going away
I'll walk this journey with you
Even when I can't find inside love for myself
I will always have love for you
Even when I over analyze everything I do
I promise I will never sit back and judge you
You are the warm drops of rain that cascade across my skin on a soft spring
day
You're the rays of sunlight that warms my skin on every summer day
You're the warmth in my heart that melts the ice when my eternal winter
seems it'll never go away
You are the changing colors of autumn that I obsess over and dream about
every single day
Without you in my life I don't think I would survive another day
My heart my soul is tormented but you calm the chaos within me.

Acceptance of Pain 'Til Midnight's End

You filled my head with lies,
Your words cut through me like a knife.
But you didn't hurt me.
You broke me down inside and ripped apart my mind.
But you couldn't change me.
If you're going to leave at least say goodbye.
At least promise me one thing.
Promise me you won't leave at midnight.
Midnight is when the true terrors come,
When the memories of my life haunt me at my bedside.
So please,
Don't break my heart at midnight.

What I See

In my memories
I see
A ghost of a child that once was,
In your head you see
A child smiling,
But that is not what I see.
I see a child crying their self to sleep,
Buried beneath blankets to ward off a monster who defiled their bedsheets.
I see a child wearing winter clothes in the summer heat.
In your head you see
A child playing carefree,
In my memories
I see
A child escaping outside in hopes they would never have to reenter the walls
of a house where a monster lived.
In your head you hear
A child laughing,
In my memories
I hear
A child attempting to cover up pain with the illusion of happiness.
The things you say you saw and heard
From a child that was me,
Those things are just wishful thinking,
Because you refuse to accept that you somehow overlooked the hurting of a
child you should have been protecting.

Unhealed Wounds

Sometimes you don't realize the pain you've buried deep inside
Or realize the wounds that haven't healed.
Sometimes you've closed your heart off to people you had love for that you
felt was to painful to feel.
You don't feel the pain until the tears flood from your eyes for the love you
held that you denied-
in efforts to shield the parts of you you wanted to survive.
Sometimes you convince yourself you're alone because it's easier than trying
to decipher who's really there.
You built a house you hide within-
afraid of letting others in,
Afraid of the possibility of pain-
the possibility of being forgotten or somehow becoming unwanted.
You convince yourself that no one is there and attempt to face existence on
your own-
afraid trusting others will erase the person you've fought to be-
the strength you've fought to build.
Afraid to let others see the pain that drowns you within-
the deepest caverns of your soul,
Trying to convince yourself those caverns are empty because an empty
person would be easier to choose to hate.
At least in your mind it's easier to deny giving yourself the love you deserve
if you make yourself believe that inside of you are empty caverns-
where no one lays within.
Afraid to be a part of a community-
because that means letting many love you when you do not know what love
from many is.

A few you let see your gaping inner wounds-
A few you trust.
But adding to that list of those you trust is something you won't allow
yourself to do.
Being kind to you is something you've struggled with for years-
Seeing what the ones who love you see in you has never been an easy feat.
The darkness of unhealed wounds tends to consume and leave behind the
feeling of defeat.
Your heart to scared of being hurt-
Convincing yourself that to deny you love is to protect the child within.
How can you heal your wounds if you are too afraid to be consumed by the
pain inside of you?

Deep in the mind of a wounded soul

Deep in the mind of a wounded soul
I find secrets left untold
Here in the space where spirits weep
I find my spirit resting in peace
Under the light of a moonlit sky
I feel the power within me rise
In this place of mystery
I see a child who once was me
Deep in the mind of a wounded soul
I find secrets left untold
Here in the space where spirits weep
I find my spirit resting in peace
Dancing a ballroom dance
I'm coupled with both life and death
I breathe in breaths of life you see
But with Death I am most happy
Deep in the mind of a wounded soul
I find secrets left untold
Here in the space where spirits weep
I find my spirit resting in peace
A place often left in silence
I come to the place of tombstones and graves
Here where no one knows just who's stories have been left untold
Deep in the mind of a wounded soul
I find secrets left untold
Here in the space where spirits weep
I find my spirit resting in peace

I hear the call of the fae who sing
They seek a reckoning
I hear the siren song began
Justice against the horrors of humanity.

The Invisibility of Loss and The Joy Found Thereafter

I grew up with only 3 people
That ever truly saw me for me
Who made me feel loved and safe
But then they died-
I felt so out of touch.
I would sit them,
On their laps and they would hold me 'til tears went away
They would hold me near
Until I came back to reality
They would keep me safe and make me feel okay,
But then they died.
2016 in February
A week before my 18th birthday,
2020 on September 9th,
And in 2021 right as the year begun.
They each left me here
On this earth
No one to make me feel seen or safe
No place to call home
That is how I felt.
I grew up with only 3 people
That ever truly saw me for me
Who made me feel loved and safe
But then they died-
I felt so out of touch
In 2022 I finally met someone

Who saw me for me
Who made me feel loved, seen, and safe
Who understood just why I am me.

"A Love which is true"

Is it so much to ask to be loved
Not that simple "I say I love you"
Not that "I say I love you back" kind of love- that's not love
I try to make it all work
I do for you day in and day out
I'm working through pain you've put me through
Yes, I know you work for me, for the kids- us
I know it's a Monday through Friday job and the weekends are your time to
relax
And you tell me to relax, but when I ask for help I get ignored or told "no"
"not now" "I'm trying to relax"
If that's the case I can't relax
Our children need someone watching them, taking care of them
My children- they- they need me
No one else can love them like me
No one else will stop their world for my babies like I do
No one will sacrifice sleep- time- energy- friends- or anything else for my
babies the way I do
And don't mistake that as me saying I don't like doing it or I don't want to
do it
I WOULD NEVER TRADE A SINGLE MOMENT WITH THEM
FOR ANYTHING!
I will never wish for what I give up for them because I rather have my babies
and know that my babies know I love them without a doubt
I'll never choose anyone or anything over my babies

I know my babies love me unconditionally and I love them unconditionally
and I love them more and more with every breathe- with every beat of my
heart
They are my life- my every breathe- my every waking moment- my every
thought- without them I am nothing no one
My babies give my life purpose and meaning-
They're the embodiment of true love
There is no love greater than that which is shared between a mother and her
children- this is the truest most pure of loves.

Secrets meant to Unfold

There is a story to be told
Secrets to unfold
Like the flickers of a flame
The things that can't be erased
You try to burn the pages
But they are flame resistant
The words scorched in your book come to life
You run with feet that never touch the ground
You speak with words that have no sound
Yet there is a story to be told
Your secrets will unfold
As your spirit dances with the flames
Your purpose cannot be erased.

Pain of Thy Soul

The depths of my soul are lonely & dark
A desolate sea of anguish with an unquenchable desire for more
I stand in a world surrounded by shadows of mere puppets
Shrouded from light by the chaos of internal torment
I search for rest with weary feet
And yet it seems no such rest exists for me
This world is as if a crowded graveyard
The greed & hate of those that rule bring nothing but death & destruction
Is my fate to forever be lost in a sea of anguish?
The dark spirals of my troubled mind swirl around me
As if caught in a whirlpool-
I almost disappear
Drowning in my own despair
The one that loathes themself is no other than I
I feel not hate for the rest of mankind
But a part of me cannot seem to find love for thyself within mine own eyes
A reflection of a lonely corpse-
Embodied by mine own spirit-
Stares back at I through the glass of time
In this mirror I see what I hate-
Mine own reflection:
A shell of a person-
Who feels lost & alone, defeated, depressed-
Someone who struggles to find internal happiness
Mine eyes are but the shadows of a painful life
MINE heart is but an unrhythmic beat of anguish that keeps no company
with time

Mine body is but rotting wood that merely falls apart with pain at a single
touch
Is it that I hate thyself?
Or do'th thou hate thine on perception of thyself?
A perception of weakness-
Someone broken & vulnerable
Do I hate that thy life could have been anything-
Yet it seems to had been destined to be full of only pain
A child cries from within
Thy inner wounds sting as if cuts exposed to salt
Internally my soul bleeds out
But safety first,
I must maintain an illusion of being okay-
As to no one find out my true pain-
Consuming me from within.

November 19th

There are words buried within
Trapped in my core-
That beg to surface
But my voice can make sense of them not
As if my mind can't comprehend what sits in my core
These words speak of desires-
Desires held within at depths unseen.

Tears

The tears ebb away at my soul
Sorrow taking hold
The emotions take reign
Their reason for being remain untold
"You have to use your words"
"Say what it is you want"
But somehow speaking of what I want in the moment
(not the bigger picture I want to see)
Makes verbalizing anything seem outside of reach
I feel the tears swell up inside
Yet they never make it to the surface
It's as if my body still retains the need clear vision played for survival
throughout the young years as I aged.
The tears drown my spirit
But dry before reaching my eyes
To feel the tears that try to escape-
Yet are kept hostage by mind
Gives feelings of
Treacherous Agony.

please don't forget

I'm here
Do you hear me calling
Do you feel my presence nearing
You're not alone
Do not fear
I'll watch over you while you release the tears
You're safe now
I know it's hard to believe
So I'll sit with you while you allow your soul to breathe
When surround silence befalls
But with solitude the agony within finds means to be released
You need to heal
Learn how to feel what it is you wish not to feel
Learn to cry without the fear of being heard
The time in life when silent tears were your saving grace is no longer
It is now safe to cry out loud
To release the hurt and pain you lock inside
It's okay to cry where you are seen
Allow others to sit with you when in sorrow's company.

World of Color

Every time I close my eyes
I see the world of color come alive
The tears portrayed by streaking hues of greys
The emotions of each person
I feel & I see the world through different sets of eyes
With every line & brushstroke
Every time I close my eyes
I see the world of color come alive
The existence of every human
Expressed through the art they choose
I feel the pain that's portrayed behind the brushstrokes with paint
Every time I close my eyes
I see pictures & patterns that stain my mind
But never find my canvas
Every time I close my eyes
I see the world of color come alive.

Not Alone

I see you
I hear you
I understand what you're going through
I know the lies in your mind
The questions of "why"
And the tears you hold inside
I'm here reaching out
Extending my hands
I'm ready to stand with you
I know what you're going through
Because I've walked a mile in your shoes
I know what it's like to not want to survive
To be beaten and raped and called out of name
To see yourself through a shattered mirror
I know-
I have been there
I know what you're going through
Because I've walked a mile in your shoes.

As A Child

As a child I felt wild but never free
I felt bound by chains of conformity
The pain that lingered called me by name
As a reminder that I would never be the same
I lost my youth before it ever began
I've lived my life attempting to outrun this
I've spent countless days wishing for an end
To myself, my pain & the trauma, that made me like this
As a child I felt wild but never free
I felt bound by the chains of conformity
I've waited decades for my life to end
Yet after decades of waiting my life finally began
I've never known just who I am
Always lost in my own reflection
The memories of pain from years ago still haunt my dreams and leave me
cold
As a child I felt wild but never free
I felt bound by the chains of conformity
But now it's time to let it go
Time to rewrite what I think I know.

No More

No day looms-
No fear holds-
Worries are no more-
For I or You-
A peace-
A tranquility-
Now takes hold and now consumes-
This light that's brought by a peaceful mind-
Gives way to heart divine-
No more anguish for the rest of your time-
Only peace & love shall journey on with You, with I.

October 19, 2018

The pain runs deeper than words My voice is locked away
I lost all words How do I speak?
How can I speak?
How do I find my voice?
Fear is the strongest emotion I feel "Run away"
"Lock yourself away"
Are the words my fear says Leave and don't look back Don't come back
But I can't
They need what I fear They need what's here
That touch use to be so calming

That touch use to erase all pain and fear
But now it's just a reminder of what it was supposed to protect me from It's
just a reminder of pain and fear
A reminder of how weak and broken I really am
This is life
A new life I haven't had in many years
My life
A life with pain and fear and hate for myself
Just when I started to love myself, I was made dirty, and hate came back
once more
The only part of me I love completely without one ounce of hate are my
children,
They are a part of me,
They are my heart and I have to move on and keep living for them no matter
how bad I want to disappear and never breathe air again
Now they are the ones I have to live for,

They're my light on the darkest of days.

221

Your Twisted Perception

To worship your god is to denounce myself,
It would be a sign of Stockholmers syndrome-
I would be running to a god who watched my torture-
One who heard my cries and refused my prayers.
You bow down to westernized religion-
You call the spirits that comfort me evil-
You say anything that lives where light it absent is of dark desire-
You call them demons-
But I know them as comforters of my weary spirit-
Those that protect me and those that answer my prayers.
You think any being that does not wish to live under your god's rule is
twisted,
Yet your god turns away from those made victims-
Your god aids those that prey on innocence-
And somehow you believe my gods and the entities that comfort me are the
evil ones.
Do you not see the reflection of your beliefs,
Do you not hear the cries of the innocents and the pain that they call out
with?
Do you honestly believe a just and fair being would idly stand by and watch
as children are tortured, as minds are shattered, as hearts sink with despair
and defeat?
How can you bow down to something so vile?
How can you truly believe it is just?
What about choosing to let horrible things happen is fair?
How is allowing a world of hate and harm exist when a being has the power
to stop it signify love?

How do you not see the monster between the scriptures?
Are you truly so brainwashed that you cannot think for yourselves?
Can you not tell wrong from right?
Just from unjust?
Love from hate?
How did those lines become so blurred?
How do you believe your god is good when its actions prove otherwise?
Can you not discern?
Are you even aware of all the passages that do not align with what you're
taught to take as truth?
You call my gods idols-
You call my comforters demons-
You call my ancestors evil-
Yet my gods, my comforters, my ancestors-
They love, guide, sooth my weary spirit-
They are the ones who tell me to keep living-
They are the ones who wipe away my tears and hold me as I cry-
They meet me in my place of brokenness with their hearts and hands
outstretched-
They pull me out of my depression-
They make me laugh when all I felt before was sorrow-
They remind me I am not alone.
Yet your god-
It never answered my prayers-
It left me in silence alone with my depression-
Alone with my thoughts-
Alone with a belt around my neck-
Alone with a closed room, gasoline, and paint thinner-
Your god told me I was not enough-
It shunned me for how I was created-
It shunned me for how and who I love-
It tortured me with its refusal to recuse me,
And you believe the beings I pray to are the evil ones?

Ahhhh How Restless I am

Restless I grow as the days draw on-
Happiness.
Content is what I search to be-
But I'm restless.
I want to do more, be more, for my kids-
Afraid of complacency-
Terrified of finding myself in a repeating cycle of feeling stuck, unmoving-
So tired of things that seem never changing-
I can't stand for things to stand still-
As I wish I could let the screams out from my internal chasm I fill with more
and more dread of the unchanging day tomorrow brings-
I journey to find myself but somehow feel like I'm losing my sanity in the
process-

To many people who feel that their thoughts should make a difference to me
or that their opinions matter, like not having their approval or choice
consent will somehow stop my world or it'll somehow matter to me-
All the while not realizing they don't make a difference to me-
Or at least if a difference is made its minimal nothing chaotropic.
I miss people I use to not have to miss-
People who I use to have friendships with & those friendships were
unbothered they mattered not to anyone else-
I don't typically miss people but when it feels like people who contributed
to life altering memories are not within reach then I do miss them-
But not those who made me feel I had to choose.

What Will Be Of History

I do'na know what is to be told
What stories will remain once this time's been buried in graves
Will stories be told
Or will we be forgotten
Who will remain
Living through words passed down from other generations
I do'na know what is to be told
Will I be remembered
Or am I to be forgotten
Will a legacy remain
Or will they burn every page
Will they attempt to erase
Or will our stories stay
I can'na say
Which way
Our histories will play
For I do'na know what is to be told.

Tears To Mine Eyes

I learn of myself with every passing day
I learn what makes me cry
The tears of joy that come from longing
Longing for one's touch
To not feel that warmth
That closeness to draw me in
This creates a painful longing
A longing I search to fill
Tears doth fill mine eyes
For I knew not how strong the longing was
Until that touch sprang tears from mine eyes
Here where love never dies
A heart overfilled with love and longing
To feel that tight embrace
Rough touch that squeezes I
To feel the touch of love's skin on mine
Doth bring tears to mine eyes.

If I Were Someone Else

Maybe I would be more beautiful if I were someone else
Maybe I wouldn't lay in bed with tears behind my eyes or lives lived in other
worlds circling my mind
In a world where I could just be myself
Be seen as my higher self
A spirit with blue skin
With a black encrusted dark blue labradorite in the space of my third eye
In a place where I didn't have to experience these human happenings
In place where my spirit could be free
Maybe I would be happier if I were someone else
Maybe I wouldn't lay in bed with tears behind my eyes or lives lived in other
worlds circling my mind
Maybe if Death would kiss me again
If she would take me into the afterlife
Maybe I wouldn't feel so lost and out of place
Maybe I'd feel that closeness that comforts me
Maybe then I'd feel just as beautiful as some humans pretend to be
But maybe I'd really see it
My own internal beauty.

If My Mind Had A Body

If my mind had a body my mind would pull it's skull apart, stretching it's face out like taffy
My mind would end its own life
My mind would decorate us with engravings that would leave us painted red
If my mind had a body it would end the life of this one that we share because it knows there more out there somewhere
"If my mind had a body" is controversial most would say
Others think because my mind sets inside this mortal casing that it constitutes as a body by which my mind douth own
But my mind is not in control it is merely what is holding space, trapped inside a casing that homes within the restless consciousnesses of spirits that mere man dare to call fragments of a shattered psyche
If my mind were to dare to control this body that belongs not to one but many within its casing my mind would dare to escape
To escape from pain it still struggles to bare
To escape from a reality that has never felt real
Yet my mind chooses to stay with the rest of us for it's slowly learning how to rewrite the teachings taught to it
My mind is learning of what it means to be loved to allow one to love us
And though it doesn't want to bury us in a hollow tomb it at times does wonder of the bliss of escape
If not for the 3 that we love and that loves us loves me I'm almost certain my mind would steal this body and aid us in shedding this casing that confines our consciousness allowing us to escape from a world we do not belong in, a world that does not feel like home.

Is This Guilt?

Sometimes I wonder why I lived to tell my story
What was the Universe's point?
To leave me alive haunted by the memories
Thoughts that refuse to leave my mind?
Shattered, Scared, Broken
A mind spiraling in and out of reality
With the fingerprints of my trauma's DNA engraved within my brain
A cold, numbing sensation that tingles the folds of the front right lobe of
my mind
The desires that conflict
Wanting to cease to exist
But wanting to exist for my wife and children
The urge to rip out every hair follicle in my head,
To peel off every layer of my own skin-
Until a new me is revealed, one who no longer has the remains of trauma
staining it-
To want to stop fighting to survive the memories
But knowing my only choice is to keep going
Can't bring myself to death at mine own hands
Spending my days impatiently waiting for yet another kiss from Death
And still as I wait, fearing the pain of disconnect from the three that tether
me to existence on this mortal plane
I can feel my body slowly dying
And I hold tight to life
Because I now have three reasons to fight to stay alive
I want to live and also die but I cannot have both at the same time
I just want the memories and pain to be erased

I don't want to remember all the awful things
I don't want to have to face the horrors that make me feel this way-
Depressed, High Anxiety, Unwanted, Unimportant,
A life that makes no difference, an annoyance- thorn in the sides of others,
A burden, Angry, hurt, lost, Unknown, misery that consumes me at the
center of my soul,
I don't want to feel-
Broken, Useless, out of place
I don't want to feel like I always have to pretend I'm okay.
Do I disappoint everyone else the same way I disappoint myself?
Why was I forced to live?
Why can't I do more?
Why is my body so sick?
Why can't I push myself to feel okay physically?
I hate myself quite often
I feel like a burden to everyone.
What difference does my existence make?
Does my life mean anything at all?
Am I failing as a spouse?
Am I a horrible parent?
Do my children truly know how much I love them?
I feel like a waste of space
Why is it so hard to love myself?
What made me worth surviving?
I constantly feel like a failure
Why do I feel so worthless?
What is wrong with me?
Why can't I bring myself to scream in silence to help release what stays
bottled up within?
Why did my cousin die from the abuse he endured but I managed to survive
mine?
Why did I live but my daughter die?
Why did I live but my Aunt Marie die?
Why did I live but my Uncle Paul die?
Why did I live but my brother die?

Why did I live but my Papa die?
If my cancer diagnosis is accurate then why am I still alive after all these
years?
Why did the Universe choose to make me survive?
What use or good am I to anyone?

"I'm scared to say"

No one else has ever searched my soul-
But when our eyes lock I can't break hold.
With you I am not alone-
All these tears I use to cry seem like distant memories when
you're by my side.
All the pain that I use to feel is now happiness that is oh so real
No one else has ever searched my soul-
But when our eyes lock I can't break hold.
All the loneliness I use to feel disappears every time you are near.
I wish I would have told you then, how much I've loved you since
we were kids-
But I was scared of losing you
Not knowing what to do-
But now I know I could never lose you-
Even if we are just friends forever & never nothing more
I'll still be happier than I was before god placed you
back in my life.
I thought what I had before was love but I was wrong,
If I had only remembered how I felt when we were young-
Then I would've seen that it wasn't so-
But god put you back in my life-
Just in time to save me not once but twice-
I'll always love you-
I'll always be in love with you-
I wish I would've told you when we were kids-
That I love you endlessly-
And even if we just stay friends-

I'll love & support you & your decisions-
Because you mean more than the world to me-
I'll always love you endlessly-
And I promise to respect all your boundaries-
'Cause I know I couldn't stand to lose you-
But I wish I would've told you when we were young-
That I've fallen hopelessly in love.

Becoming the In-between

Under the surface there is a whirlwind of emotions-
Under the surface words take over this world-
Under the surface reality no longer exists-
Under the surface love is no longer a distant shore-
But,
On the surface porcelain fields portray perfect paintings-
On the surface love is never said in fear of a broken heart-
On the surface a mask covers the true identity-
On the surface it is possible to run to safety while running from the truth-
Yet,

Some have merged the surface with what's underneath-
This creates a place where porcelain fields portray emotions instead of
perfect paintings-
Where love is more than a word and takes away the fear of a broken heart,
Changing the world-
Where the masks no longer exist, and the identity becomes one with reality-
Where love isn't ran from and is possible because it is now seen as safe and
true-
No longer trapped between the surface and what's underneath.

Nothing I Dread

There is nothing I dread-
For there are opportunities in every occasion-
When the sun rises and a new day begins-
I rejoice-
With nothing to dread.
Life is what you allow it to be-
And if you spend all your days dreading what is or is to come-
Then your life will be hollow and empty.
So, there is nothing I dread.

The Story

This is the story of a lover who was told not to cry-
A child who loved them self before all the lies-
This is the story of a mother who can't sleep at night-
A woman haunted by the memories in her mind-
This is the story of a boy who grew up alone-
Searching for a place his heart could call home-
This is the story of the people left unheard-
The voices pushed into silence then called absurd-
This is the story of a generation making change-
Ones who refuse to be erased.

Empathy

I know not what you speak of only what you feel inside
I feel the energy pass from you to me and I'm undone
My mind unravels
Emotions entwined
I thought the bouts of depression where over but now I feel yours as if
they're mine
To feel emotions not meant to be mine
To feel the thoughts you hold inside
I think of ways to stop the energy flow of emotions that pass in between
Yet I want to help walk you through the sea of overbearing emotions you
swim through
Underneath the surface that you petrary as "fine" I can feel what it is you
work to hide
Your words do not match the emotions you lock inside
You attempt to paint over the chaos you hold within
You attempt to push down the feelings that are too strong to fight
You look around feeling as if no one would care but do you see me?
I'm here
I feel your emotions though they are not mine
I feel the emotions tied to the thoughts you hold inside
I once longed to sever the flow that passes in between
But now I realize to be seen and understood is what it is you need
Below the surface you feel alone feeling as if you are standing on the outside
of life
You feel as if you're watching life take place
You feel as if you'll never actually participate
You feel as if you're invisible

You don't see me because I'm standing on the outside with you as you watch
I feel what you're feeling
Will you step back from your viewing spot?
Will you take a moment to realize you're not alone?
I once stood where you are standing
Not realizing I was isolating myself as you're doing now
There are layers to what your feeling
So please let me help
Let me help ease the pain
Just talk to me
About anything
There is time to peel back each layer of pain but let's start slowly as you learn
the way
Healing is a journey
So don't be afraid
It's okay if have to go back to layers that you thought were fully peeled away
You're a living being
Which means sometimes the peels come back like skin growing over a
wound
Sometimes shedding the peels of pain reveals scars
That to is okay don't be ashamed
We all live with something that has left its mark
You're perfect just as you are regardless of if you have one or countless scars
Just because the world seems unforgiving doesn't mean you can't have
self-compassion
In fact self-compassion is the first step to self-love
You have to learn to give yourself compassion
To see yourself
To meet yourself
Right where you are
I thought the bouts of depression where over but now I feel yours as if
they're mine
I'm here
I feel what you're feeling

There is time to peel back each layer of pain but let's start slowly as you learn
the way
to healing, to having self-compassion.

239

Palestine, My Heart with Thee

Seeing the images of explosions in the sky
Hearing the voices of the men, women, and children cry
The look of pain painting their eyes
It's as if my heart is being ripped from my chest, dissected, then minced as
Palestinians die
What horrors the Israeli government seeks to justify when there is no
justifying taking innocent life
The governments funding the unjust are just as guilty, just as inhumane
To know, to see what is being done my spirit fills with pain and grief
Tears stream from my eyes as I wish I had the power to bring the
Palestinians relief
The Palestinians cry for freedom and peace yet Israel spreads false narratives
of war
First Palestine is stolen then it's people tortured, killed
When will the trauma cease
Israel is not a state that should stand
Israel is the land known as Palestine which belongs to Palestinians
The killings must stop, the horrors must end, there is no justifiable reason
for the inhumane treatment of those who are suffering at Israel's hands
All the world needs to take a stand
Embrace one another
Stand hand and hand
Raise our voices
Free Palestine, Free Palestinians.

A Realm Unseen

241

Remembered After Death

Sometimes I wish upon a star
Sometimes I wonder where you are
People say I can't remember everyone that I love who has died
But I remember them
For me it keeps them alive
I remember
Lover Baby my kitten so sweet who died in my hands as I held him and
watched him take his last breath
Gentle my puppy who probably never stood chance he was born with a
green stomach
Stephen and Micah friends from my childhood
Sky my dog who protected me and made me feel safe and loved
Aunt Miemie my aunt who taught me healing
Aunt Kay and Uncle Hermen she was a high priestess and he her husband
I remember
Uncle Paul who taught me algebra and supported my every journey
My brother Daniel who shared his humor by passing thoughts to me as if we
could communicate telepathically
Papa my great grandpa who was a father to me showing me what patience
was and loving me
Marieah my daughter who never took a single breath who died inside me
Coach Wright who always encouraged me and gave me confidence to face
my surroundings
Rainbow and Minnow our two fish from childhood
Mrs. Smith the neighbor of my great grandparents
Sue who was always kind
My cousin Eli who died at 3 way before his time

My cousin Skylar who I've only seen pictures of
My grandpa Gene who was always talking about some kind of Christian
based conspiracy
I remember
Uncle Paul from another family but was like my own family he was funny he
was kind he made me smile every time I saw him at their family get
togethers
My great grandmother who died before I can remember
But I remember stories and I have talked to her spirit
As her spirit sat next to me
I remember the death of many people
I feel connected to the realm of Spirits
I know they're still out there
And remembering them keeps them alive to me
Keeps them alive for all eternity
I will not forget them or who they are
Or what I have learned from learned from them
I will not forget the ways they changed lives
I remember the ones others forget
I see and hear their spirits.

Spirits' Sorrows Left Untold

Once died I

Now alive I roam

To free the spirits entombed by sorrows that were left untold

To be the eyes

To be the ears

To feel the pain that traps them here

I prefer the company of the dead

So I continue through the land

In search of spirits yet to leave

In hopes I can help to set them free.

The Spirits Around Me

Ready to leave this earth
To travel to planets far beyond what is known to humans
Expansion of the mind can be felt throbbing within as my spirit attempts to
escape this bleak human existence
My spirit growing and expanding past the point of an orbiting planet I feel
trapped on
No this isn't depression
No this isn't mind sickness
No this isn't a wish for the afterlife
Just a yearning to step between the worlds of existence without the shackles
of the veil standing in between me and this mundane experience
The human corpse ebbs away slowly
I feel the physical sicknesses that haunt it and I feel the spiritual freedom
beckoning me to let this corpse wilt away as if an entirely different body
awaits
I feel, I sense my being shifting as if a caterpillar metamorphosing into a
butterfly
I sense a change awaiting as if something is within reach yet unseen to my
eyes
I feel the pressure and throbbing of my pineal gland as I sense these changes
as I feel a pull of a rope I cannot see
My heart shatters and mends all within the same breath and the lives of the
spirits around me call for me to sit and stay to listen to the lessons they've
learned while living- to show me their spirits' minds so that I might not
succumb to the same hands of fate

The spirits ask me to open myself fully but still caution holds my reigns for what will become of me if my spirit steps outside this corpse to defy the laws placed on it by mere man
The voices of the earth cry out asking to be touched by hands of love and healing to bring to it the spirits it birthed for change, and she calls to me in the day and also within the night to lay with her to create love with her to put to bed the man-made fears that no longer hold purpose but still whisper in my ears
The earth she calls to me gently but fiercely never a whisper but more a wail-
Nearly a painful screaming that draws me into the night-
Calling me to bask beneath the moon to breath in her very breathe-
To make myself one with her as she intended upon the day of my creation
And the spirits that have painted my path cry for me to realize it wasn't meant as a curse but as a gift-
To open all of my senses to a journey I was meant to travel-
A journey I once thought I was destined to have to travel alone,
And as the spirits make known their plans they show me I was sent love of such purity not just to feel and to give but to receive from the children I bore to the spirit in which mine has become entwined to,
A love that is known to never end nor leave and here the spirits call me to trust fully so they may make known all in which they have crafted me and my life to be
And yet I sit in the wind hearing her voice the voice of my mother the earth and I feel her spirit surrounding me attempting to ease my earthly pains-
To wipe away the sorrows that leak from my mortal eyes as she lulls sweet songs to me of the days in which I'll see all I am capable of without doubting or thinking maybe this person the world sees is just mad-
Crazed due to life's events in which I felt as if I was played as a puppet for a twisted god's amusement,
And here she calms me-
Dear sweet Mother Earth mourns with me the broken and hurting heart her child holds-
Only wishing her child could see the beauty of the painting she has created with every breath she has ever breathed,
My spirit cries as if it's age is held outside of time-

As if it has lived to many lives to count-
And here the earth tells me it's true my spirit's age no number can count,
She sings me sweet songs that only her voice can carry-
They're sweet whispers known as wind and as she breathes her songs into me my spirit it expands-
For no story man can make up could ever erase the touch of earth's hands
So I sit and I cry feeling the emotions of all the lands-
And I feel sorrow of lost spirits and those of wondering man-
And here as the sorrows of every living thing fills up inside me the spirits meant to guide my path both sit and stand amongst me-
Close enough for me to feel but too far away for me to see-
For they know my spirit is ready but this corpse's mind still needs more healing-
So they stay close enough to make their selves known but faraway enough to stay hidden from my eyes-
And as I feel the spirits around me I feel both tense and at ease,
I feel tense for I know not what they want to say or better yet what stories they wish to show me-
And I feel at ease because throughout my life I've felt utterly and completely alone and I no longer feel as if I'm invisible in a world full of people who are seen,
The spirits that journey with me keep me in peaceful company-
And I know that with my loves and the spirits around me I shall never more be alone,
I'll always have a helping hand reaching out and guiding lights to lead me along my life's path,
So I ask-
Oh Mother Earth and spirits of those who were before me-
All that wish well-
All those with good intentions-
Please help me to heal what needs healed within myself for I wish nothing more than to be one with my spirit-
I wish not to feel this small divide as if a seam has been sewn between my spirit and my mind,
I wish for my spirit and my mind to be as one fully entwined.

When Spirit and Heart Talk

When you haven't known someone for long, but you feel like your soul has journeyed with theirs for many lifetimes before-

When you think you know happiness, but then you met this person and somehow in one day's time you feel like what you thought happiness was doesn't even begin to scratch the surface of what happiness feels like with this person-

When you think I'll never find someone who understands every part of me, everything I've seen and been through, but then this person comes along and they understand it all-

When you think it's only you who sees through these lenses, but then you met this person and it's as if you and them have been looking through the same pair of eyes all your lives-

When you had once convinced yourself, you'll just have to force yourself to be okay with whomever you end up with one day, but then you met this person and

every part of your mind, body, and soul is drawn to them and just one look from them, one smile from them, makes you feel this unexplainable way it's a strong feeling something you've never felt before-

When you question if how you feel matters and if you'll ever find someone you can be fully you with, but then you met this person and all your walls disappear with them and all of a sudden you can't hold back how you feel, you can't hold back who you are because they make the real whole you shine through-
When your whole life you've been taught to question everything, but then this person comes along and you don't feel a need to question anything-

When you once questioned instant connections and past lives, but then you met this person and you feel an instant connection unlike any connection you've ever felt before and all of a sudden you feel like knowing this person in past lives is the only explanation for all of this, you think to yourself maybe we were together in every life before this-

When you met this person, and you can feel your ancestors at peace like they've finally guided you to where you need to be, and they can finally rest knowing you've found the path the Great Spirit designed for you to live-

When you finally feel at complete peace like you've found your forever person, someone you can connect with, someone you can relate to, someone who understands everything, someone who is everything you could ever possibly imagine but yet also so much more than you could ever imagine.

When all there is hope for a wonderful and beautiful future together and you wonder when everything else will happen, but you're also not worried because you just know that this person was created for you, and you were created for this person.

Spirits Trapped

I travel with reapers at my sides as they guide spirits to their afterlives
Spirits trapped call to me
They show me their worst memories
Spirits who once lived feeling unseen, unheard, and never found
They come to me
They seek me out
Here they sit
Here they stand
They share their pain as their memories begin to play
In my mind my sight they overtake
As the truth their story within me plays
To bring them peace
To help them rest
I will take and hold onto their pain and memories
As reapers search I search not
For my spirit cast a beckon for spirits trapped and spirits lost.

The Spirits My Friends

I am of a higher dimension
I call the spirits my friends
The spirits stand with me on the battlefield
We walk together hand-and-hand
I travel through time simply by entering my mind
I see the past, present, and future
And I feel what needs to be healed
I am one with the ocean,
One with the land and the sky
I am one with the spirits
I travel between both sides of life
I have tasted death
And been brought back to life
I am from higher dimensions
I call the spirits my friends
And in an open field the spirits dance with me hand-and-hand
The spirits I call friends to me stand around me
The spirits surround me with an ancient covering
I once had walls built to the sky to protect me
As a child these walls crumbled to my feet
Where I once saw beauty across the land I then saw suffering
But now I stand beside the remains of the walls that crumbled to my feet
No more secrets
No more pain
These walls I now rebuild again
I mix the mortar with my words
And the clay with memories

I build these walls not to shield but to reveal everything
Everything that shame once held
The spirits I call my friends they surround me with an ancient covering
I have tasted death
And the spirits brought me back to life
I call the spirits friends to me
And the spirits call me something I have never been called before
The spirits call to me
They call me by a name they gave to me
The spirits I call my friends
They call me Spirit Walker
For I walk between the worlds I see... every side... of everything.

To Teether Between

The screams fall on silent ears and whispers die on numb hearts never
reaching the untouched hand

To feel the sorrow of the nations
To hold within a pain unfound-
To know the troubles of unrested souls
Begs to bargain between two worlds
A world only some may see and a world most think they live within

Never realizing their world has swallowed them whole devouring their
essence leaving them without their soul

To be drawn to and to teether between two worlds
Both at times seen but unseen
One may feel as if they hold unbearable pain within their soul
A soul destined for more than a bleak existence
Nothing mortal ever feeling enough yet left to feel crazed by mortal
restraints
And here we hear the spirits' whispers and are surrounded by the mute
man's screams.

Mad Man's World

It's a mad man's world don't you see?
To live outside of harmony
To feel not complete
To not know or understand true love or peace

And yet robotic people belonging to the grand puppeteer vainly wonder
why they feel as if an empty vase untouched and unnoticed by the people in
the room

To live a life outside existence is to not exist at all

Though one may walk down narrow halls, the only ones to hear their steps is
clearly known to be their self

For other puppets have not the ears to hear each other's steps

Nor the eyes to take notice of the stringed creation that walks beside them
For each puppet is missing what it takes to sense the world around it

Each left feeling crazed as tangled strings leave them to hang in a mad man's
world where there's no vision day or night

They hang blind, deaf, mute, and numb to the world that lies within them
all, because the puppeteer has said they're each nothing in life without him.

Left Unfolding

I don't expect anyone to understand things in which they have not endured
Nor do I expect one to understand or believe the things in which they have
not experienced or seen
Though my age may say I have much to learn it speaks not for what I've
endured nor the things in which I've seen

My age speaks not for what I know or what I feel in spirit as truth
Nor does my age paint an accurate description of the things made known to
thee

Age tells nothing of the lessons I've learned through my life and lives of
others

So, for anyone to assume my age tells all one needs to know I'll set back and
watch your life unfold ne'er once attempting to tilt the scale
For if you know all need of me by the age accompanying me then I shall not
lend a hand or attempt to share what I know
I'll prove your point and sit back idly as your spirit's history repeats itself
and you yet again fail to see the lessons ladened in the land meant to bring
new life to what I see you as- another dying man.

A Soul Lost

A soul lost in the abyss of mortality,
Knowing all to be gained or all to be lost for either a moment or all of
eternity.
The question still remains,
It still beckons from within,
Do'th the pain ev'r subside,
Or do'th pain continue its course.
Here ly'th the remains of a tomb unrobbed of pain,
A mortal corpse,
A bag of bones,
A life full of both loss and gain.
The human existence 'tis full of pain,
Life seemly cherished and also somehow remaining bleak.
To live is to know you must one day die,
Somehow life is lived on borrowed time,
Though time is a construct of the human mind,
Mortal life is shackled to this false construction that continually divides.
What pain one soul do'th feel as it searches for what is real,
When it finds the truth it holds on tight,
But truth both frees and burdens the mind,
For any corpse belonging to a soul that has learned the truths man withhold
finds itself in a place where society is seen as chains,
Truth calls to erase the constructs that do not belong,
What is unnatural is that which was created to control.
Are people not but caged and tortured animals,
Do we not search for an escape?
To find the place our soul calls home,

To be one with the nature surrounding us,
To be free and not controlled?
What pain we now feel as hidden truths become revealed,
To know the lies that kept us here,
To be stuck in a place without escape,
How do we find a way out of here?
I call out from the abyss.
My soul tortured now finding bliss,
But first I must escape this prison with invisible chains,
I must escape society,
So I may truly become free.
My soul calls from the abyss,
Not for light,
Not to escape the dark,
But rather to find the truth and get out of a society that wills those like me
to their tomb.

The Garden Beneath Tears

My tears fall where they cannot be seen,
My cries drowned out by the sound of water filling porcelain,
As I rock back and forth, I question my own existence,
I question my worth and purpose.
My heart feels hollow as if infected by an opened wound,
This need- this desire- for love and affection that seems no mortal can fulfil.
Here where my hopeless reflection stares back at me-
My thoughts flow-surrounding me like the water burning skin-
I see the patterns- I know them well-
And still, I sit here questioning if life on earth is the true hell.
But then as my tears run out no more liquid spilling from my eyes-
Solace finds me as I began to forget this physical realm,
The sorrow- the pain- drives me from this world,
Peace finds me where the spirits dwell.
Gods and spirits enter that space where it's just me, hot water, and an empty
place.
My tears carried prayers to ancient gods-
I was heard and answered from the beyond.
The love I desired fulfilled where my spirit met with the gods-
Always at the exact time of need-
And there our spirits dance- entwine-
A garden of great divine-
A garden where I give myself as offering as shrine.
Entwining spirits reaches beyond the torture of mortality-
For even death does not divide the peace of these in which create a unity.

Letters To My Gods

Loki

Your humor,

Your tricks,

Always come at the right time-

Just as your calm finds me in the midst of emotional torment.

You sit with me until I am fine,

By my side when I wish for death-

You remind me life is to live.

Your presence has become one associated with a grandfather,

Not for age but for your personality and comfort.

Hel

You are as a mother to me,

I find rest even in my thoughts of you.

A peace within your presence I feel.

Though in a place of afterlife

You surround me with warmth to thaw my heart which slowly freezes.

Freya

Your strength gives me strength,

Your advice I heed,

I call you Aunt because I feel safety with thee.

Athena

I have long come to You,

Your wisdom and strategies have provided survival.

Your love for art has blossomed within in for a while.

Aphrodite

Through You I learn how to love myself,

I have slowly learned to see beauty within myself.

Without you I do not know if I would have ever learned selflove at all.
Selene
You provide solace as I sit surrounded by moonbeams,
You are the first goddess I ever connected with,
The first deity I ever gave my heart to,
All those years ago in my youth-
I found solace in simply knowing you.
Through the years you have held my heart and comforted me when I fell
apart.
Lilith
You have taught me of the power within myself,
You taught to see my true self,
Some say they fear you, but I only feel love.
And your beauty draws me into the depths of your mysteries.
Hecate
You have left signs for me to find- all throughout my life,
I knew not then what I know now,
My fascination with keys, dividing paths along the road, the power of magic
sourced from within-
You have been with me even when I did not know.
Morrigan
You have always been at my favorite place-
The place I met the best of friends-
To know now that You had been there watching over me-
Always calling my spirit to journey back to those at the cemetery.
Ishtar/Ianna
You taught me gods/goddesses they see-
The struggles of mortality,
You understand the hardships of this physical existence.
And my life is not about the gender others perceive but rather who I feel
myself to be.
Death
The spirit of a woman is how You come to me,
Your presence is oh so comforting,
I remanence on our encounter-

The day we first met and how your decision has altered my perception of existence.
You chose to bring me back to this mortal plane,
Things left to do some would say,
I remember the spirts I met as You stood behind me knowing theirs and my meeting would be brief.
And still, I call to you-
To sit with me when I feel my body is a mortal tomb.
My second love-
This love is deeper than the one from my youth,
This love continuously beckons me to You.
I miss your touch, your embrace-
"Kissed by death" a common read phrase, yet it rings true for You and I,
And when our lips meet once more time will no longer divide.
My words to You are the longest here-
You've changed my life beyond change of years.
Death I love You-
I miss You so-
Yet as You and I both know,
'Tis not the time to reunite,
I have my children,
I have my wife,
But when the day comes or maybe night in which we reunite-
I'll hold on tight,
If by then those I now love are already by your side.
To dance with You is to dance in grace,
You will always be my favorite shade of Grey.

In the Ringing I hear

Stay focused
Gathering new.
Spirit's wise (wise belonging to one's spirit- my spirit?)
Flowers bloom-
Gardens grow-
The path entwines what the spirit births to grow.
I see you in what you feel is weak and frail-
The broken pieces are the sharpest tools to use to build,
Mirrors are merely reflections of what we don't want to see or don't want to
be-
Not truth but fear painted glass-
Designed to reflect back insecurities and broken mindsets in order to
sustain a shattered reality binding those in the glass to enslavement
disguised as freedom,
I whisper to you-
Look not in the glass nor in reflections of water,
The water is to wash away what needs not to be there,
Do not take back what had been cleansed from you by looking at its
reflection,
Reflections will always try to reattach.
Time cannot end-
Only things with beginnings can end-
And if it's true time has always been-
Then it serves to say time hath no beginning and therefore where there is no
beginning there too lays no end.
The willow weeps to my spirit and my tongue cannot find the words to
translate the tears of the willow that is wept upon me.

The oak stands tall in solitude and my spirit knows not how to say what the
great oak says to it-
But here in its branches my spirit find safety-
A place to hid-
A place to rest.
The wind whispers to my spirit and my spirit spreads it's wings and begins to
fly-
Fly to where the laughter never ends-
And to the place the crying heart felt there was only dread,
The wind whispers healing and carries memories.
The stream dances over dirt and rocks teaching my spirit the true feeling of
freedom-
And sweeps the current under me revealing a world I had never seen.

Death's Kiss

I don't want to feel alive-
I just want to feel alright-
I don't want to be dead-
I just want to want to feel that feeling I once felt-
The peaceful bliss of Death's kiss-
People say they feel dead inside-
As way to explain that they're depressed-
But for me to explain the torture felt when depresses-
I would have to explain it as feeling too alive inside-
Depression hurts-
Depression is full of sorrow & agony-
But the kiss of Death is sweet with peace-
There's a sense of bliss that Death's dark void brings-
The nothingness washes over leaving you with an unexplainable peace-
Feeling calm-
All fear gone-
All pain erased-
No more torture or agony.
This is why I say-
I don't want to feel alive-
I just want to feel alright.

The Night of the Waxing Gibbous

The moon calls to me from a cloudless sky
The yellow orange of cat eyes,
The waxing gibbous of the early darkened day
3:17 am the numbers say.
The moon draws me in as if I can fly to meet with it
My feet long to touch its surface,
Something in me feels life on it,
Or maybe in it.
I'm drawn to the places we're told mortals cannot survive
Something in me either longs to prove them wrong or maybe a piece of me
longs to die,
The moon slowly creeps down from the sky to hide behind the trees in the
distance that create a line.
The more my insides cry to escape the earth
The more my spirit dares to journey beyond this universe,
The moon seems to disappear faster as if to say I may miss my chance if I
don't seize the moment that's drawing nearer.
And in this longing to journey beyond I'm reminded of the dreams from
when I was young
The dreams where I would run and jump and as I enter the air I would
somehow find flight to places I wished to be,
Away from a torturous reality.
In one dream I flew as a fictitious witch high above houses on a broom stick
I did not know then what I know now,
But still I feel trapped somewhere my spirit was never truly meant to be.
The waxing gibbous I had just seen has melted away leaving an empty sky
and with it it left an empty space within my insides,

As September nears I feel the veil thinning slowly
The veil awaits October's closing.
I wait though the waiting is impatient
All year I'm surrounded by mortals unwilling to change what they have the
power to,
Insisting on constantly complaining.
I long for the magic of moon beams to touch the two plains in
synchronicity,
For spirits to be given form for all to see
I miss those that for many years contacted me.
I miss the dead,
The dead are and have always been my dearest and best of friends.

Mystery Shrouds

A mystery shrouds a darkened mind
The folds go deep into your mind
The more you know the deeper the folds
Yet some remained chained to time
Spirits have not an age
Only lessons through memories laid
Here with a mortal shell
Our spirits must break free of ego's hell
Some do manage to escape the fate this plain exists to create
Yet some never see the light that guides others to their escape.

Lessons of The Spider's Web

The memories rush in like a story reread throughout childhood-
A book from my youth I thought had faded-
But this book ladened with atrocities had only buried itself.
Like a spider crawling into a hidden space to hide within the shadows
Somehow preserving the parts of me remaining unshielded in the place
where the sun attempted to burn holes through my flesh.
The sun slowly burning me,
The sun longing to illuminate the places where my inner spiders crept.
To reveal the story books that my psyche had banned me from looking at-
Somewhere within where spiders crept through secret shadows was answers.
Answers to the reasoning behind thoughts, concerns, and fears.
The dark fog making up the pages of those hidden books latched onto my
soul unwilling to move-
Knowing that the slow burning flames of the sun would teach me how to
disperse the painful gases of the foggy pages that suffocated me at my
depths.
The books were fire resistant yet burned me from within,
The soot of the books' flames poisoned my veins,
A sickness of sorrow and fear I didn't know could be removed or replaced.
The spiders hid from the world weaving webs in these flames,
Attempting to write new stories to put out the old books' flames.
These are the teachings I learned today as I watch a spider crawl into a
darkened space.
Each creature
Each essence
That I am willing to bare witness of-
Has a lesson it lends to the open ones.

The shadows are dark because they remain closed.
The only way to heal is to open the old books and turn the next page-
Allowing the sun to bring forth the memories of chiseled words from old days.
The words etched in each page they cannot fade but the pain they seek to bury within can be vanquished in sun rays.
The ban placed on these books of old memories they don't heal the spirit they don't set the mind free.
The bans they serve as cation tap,
Warning you through lies that acceptance nor love will ever be found in depths of this place.
The ban is there as a way to blind.
So creep little spiders and spin your webs-
Write a new book for me within,
Write the words within your webs-
Tell the story of how the gas flames of old memories could not survive once I let the sun into the shadows where the old books burned.
Write of the truths I have learned.
Of how I tore down the cation tape that stretched out within,
Weave webs of stories of the lies I've defeated,
Tell of the pain that I endured but be sure that you write of the lessons I learned.
The lesson that paved way towards those victories,
Do not just weave that I overcame.
But tell in detail so others can read your words and find freedom within-
So they too can put out the flames of old books their psyche buried deep within.

Willing "Eyes"

Fully submerged
Completely surrounded
Nature calls out
The spirits call beckoning for me to stay

To stay & play yet another game
A game of memories

They beckon for me to stay
To hold onto fleeting moments
For each moment tells a story
Holds a story that they cry out to share

The spirits cry for understanding eyes that will welcome visions of times
before their creation
Eyes that will not hide from the things the spirits wish to show them
Eyes that hold a longing to understand & to heal
Eyes that will not turn away in fear

The spirits cry for eyes willing to be fully submerged in memories that are
not their own
Eyes that welcome the spirits into their space
Eyes willing to be completely surrounded by the happiness & pain that each
spirit has felt.

"Whispers in the Wind"

The wind whispers gently telling me of days when peace covered the lands-
She calls to me to step out on a journey-
A journey to learn & find who I have been created to become-
This whisper I know well-
It's the breath of the Creator-
The mixing of two spirits-
That of Mother Earth & of Father Sky
I feel the touch of a kiss on my cheeks-
Soft & sweet-
A reminder that the Creator has not forgotten me-
A reminder that the Creator walks with me-
Side by side-
As if walking through a peaceful meadow with running streams and dancing
spirits
The wind is the voice of the one who guides with delicate direction
She speaks through the dancing leaves that live on the trees
And Father Sky shines his light down on me to illuminate the path
Mother Earth has pointed out-
The path the Creator whispers for me to journey down
And in the stillness of the day-
Way is made for the beauties of the night
Where Father Sky will shine down through beams of moonlight
For the Creator's path is never hidden-
The path is always made known-
Easy to see when you listen to the whisper of the wind that echoes in your
heart-
The whisper that rests within your spirit.

Because even spirits need to heal.

Wanting Peace While Alive

What chaos doth reside within in which continuous questions surface,
The chaos seems ne'er to subside only sway between that which can be bared
and that
which cannot.
Left to question one's own existence or merely question why one exists at all,
Here I stand dare not sit for I wish not to become insnared by the questions
the
internal chaos pose,
So how doth one lay to rest the chaos that within doth swirl?
Have ye learned any tricks that could help thee?
Please, fear not the questions I ask, I wish only for enlightening.
Do tell kind soul to me the secrets in which your journey hath unfold-
Tell thee what ye did learn during your time alive-
Tell thee the secrets that your spirit unearthed after creation left thou
nostrils-
Please Oh Please kind spirits hear and answer me.
I come to you at a time the chaos bid me lost-
A time in which I desire and long to overcome-
Kind spirits do not act like you're not there for I have seen you standing and
heard
your words many times before-
You've shown me your memories and shared with me your pain-
So please, share with me how to erase my pain-
How to make the chaos and its questions subside from within.
I long to feel peace once more-
I long to feel peace in the world of the living not just in the place that Death
resides.

Hearts of Healers

Do'st thou truly love
How douth one know the true heart's desire
Will'st I see tomorrow or 'ever be shackled in todays
Douth ye vainly exclaim one's love
Or will'st love proclaim to feel the same
Thou heart and spirit douth whisper day and night
Ye bid to rest one's heart's lullabyes
To feel as if a void succumb
For what be unseen that beckons-
Calling thee
Voices of departed souls dig away-
Stories buried that were left untold
And here thee sits
And here thee hears
The voices ringing out to spirit healers ears
The spirits dance in hearts of healers
Spirits cry on shoulders that carry the weight of many lives before them
Will'st thee join the spirits in solitude
Or do'st thou turn to face away-
To try to blend in with a world unwelcoming to them.

Of Fae and Friends

There was a time when no one knew or saw the friends I called my own
A time before I was told the Otherworld was fantasy
Before I had to pretend not to believe
A time when I carried objects with me
Gifts I had received
The gifts in which only I and those of the Otherworld could see
A suitcase of likes in which allowed one to conjure whatever they may need
This gift indeed came in hand when my friends did call on me
The day they came in search of me
They knew not what else they could do
So they came to me and told me of the horrors and atrocities
They told me of their captured friends
The cages in which they were kept
They said they couldn't find the keys in which they would need that's why
they came to me
I opened that suitcase and a great light shown
As behind me my seven shadows did appear
I knew the keys they needed where somewhere in the universe so I reached
within and pulled them out
A ring of bronze and brass keys
I handed to my friends
They thanked me kindly and left to free our friends that were stuck in
captivity
Since that day I have seen
3 golden speckled pearls
Or so I see upon the skin in color of 3 friends that watch over me from the
Otherworld

I miss my eyes of childhood
The lack of fear when sharing what I knew
For as a child earthly folk hid my truths behind the ruse of a word they
often used
Keeping my truths locked away
They called my truth a Fairytale
And insisted I forget
They told me to grow up and to stop imagining what isn't real
But I knew then and know today
The Otherworld in fact exists
Earthly folk just don't like what they do not know
Or rather what they cannot control
But just because one does not like does not mean what they dislike does not
exist
It simply means they choose to be blind to the beauty that comes from what
is different.

The Willow In Me

From pain deep within
The hollow willow weeps
It sings of times before the pain as wind whispers tales of comforts
throughout its leaves
The hollow willow cries
For it sings of a time it does not remember
A time before memories imprint in one's mind
The hollow willow aches
For pain has yet to release
A pain that wraps around its roots and refuses to leave
The hollow willow sees
Though others see a willow standing tall
No one but the hollow willow knows that the willow feels hollow
Others gaze upon the willow in awe seeing it stand tall and strong
Others see a willow who has survived harsh seasons and tells of a time with
rings within its trunk
Here the willow stands yet feels hollow and bent
Not seeing what others find awe in
Rather seeing only the memories etched in it bark and feeling the pain that
wraps around it at its roots
Here the hollow willow weeps
Cries out from within
Aches with pain it cannot describe
And sees itself through pain dowsed bark
Only wishing for both pain and memory of pain to cease surrounds it
To be free of what leaves it feeling hollow and weak.

My Spell to You

My spell to you is the song I sing-

Take a breath and release-
Anger holds no more space-

Breathe in the breath of tranquility-

I will never leave you-
Even when death comes for me-

My spirit will stay by your side-

I will guide you through all of life-

My love I share with you-
Bring peace & tranquility.

Akashic Room

I see a room-
A library some would say-

This place I see tells of no graves-

Scrolls, books, words from across all time-
Across every universe-

The knowledge, understanding, and wisdom at my fingertips-

My power-
My magic-

Flows from within & seats itself in my palms-

I hold all things as if a book to which all I wish & need to know-
Is forever in my hold.

A Time Before

Somewhere in the solace of the broken hearted

There's a peace that washes over the soul

In a meadow of memories and shadows

There's two lovers that lay side-by-side

In a time before trust became an empty promise

Before the meadow filled with lies.

"Destined To Part"

There was once a maiden-
Who sailed across seas-
Looking to find things she had never seen-
She wondered,
She walked-
Across distant shores-
Her heart in one hand-
The other an ore-
She swam & she sailed-
She walked & she climbed-
Until she felt she could journey no more-
And there in that place-
That place where she closed her eyes-
That is where her hope died-
Unknown to her-
Another was climbing up to that place-
A person that woman had never seen-
As her eyes opened from a restless slumber-
She saw the face of her destined lover-
She felt the beating of their hearts-
As she looked down she saw they carried their heart-
They carried their heart in one hand and a staff in the other-
As they each stretched out their hands-
With their hearts-
The two lovers met though destined to part-
This is the story of two lovers-
Destined to meet-

You know the lovers as land & sea-
The shores where the sea touches the land-
This is the place where they extend their hearts in their hands.

282

Land Of Dissociation

Polymer in the Mirror

Who am I?
Why am I here?
Standing-
Searching in the mirror-
For a clue as to who I am.
Why is there no face?
Why am I nobody?
Looking into glass-
No face or mask-
To show who I am,
I see a blank canvas-
No eyes-
No nose-
No mouth,
I see an empty mold before me.
What will become of me?
When I finally see-
The face in the mirror,
Not just the polymer.
Who am I
Standing here
Searching in the mirror
Why do I feel drawn
To search the glass that is hung
Why do I feel less than most?
Why do I still not know the faceless clay before me?
What secrets does the mirror hold?

My wants?
My fears?
The things untold?
Obsidian, dark as night
Show me who I am tonight
As I search your broken glass
Guide me,
Teach me,
Remove my fright
Stone of old mix with new
Help me find my truth
Mirror mirror on the wall
Hardened stone black to all
Reflect to me my secrets
Show me who I am to be
Give name,
Give face,
Give guidance
Protect me from the pain I've felt
Protect me from those with doubt
Reflect to me my spirit's face
Shield me from this mortal place
I want not to be in this realm this place
I want to find peace
To go back to a place unseen
A place unseen by mortal eyes
The place spirits reside
To live once more after death
Fills my heart with tears at best
I miss the peace I had-
No pain,
No torture,
Nothing bad
But now I live for those I love
But I will always long

For the peace that comes from death
A peace that in mortality does not exist.

286

My Own Reflection

Sometimes I wonder what its like
To know exactly who you are
Without feeling shattered or torn
Just when I feel who I am
Makes sense to me
I hear the voices in my head
The names of faces this world will never see
The people with whom I share my reality
The people who live in my body
Sometimes I wonder what its like
To not always feel like there's chaos inside
To not look in the mirror and wonder who I am
Not knowing my own reflection
Not knowing my own reflection
Every time I open my eyes I wonder
I wonder who I am
Will I remember today or will it all be erased
Will I know who they are
Will there be memories to replay
Every time I close my eyes
I never know will I wake tomorrow
Every time I close my eyes
I wonder if I'm saying goodbye
Sometimes I wonder what its like
To know exactly who you are
Without feeling shattered or torn
To not feel like there's always

Chaos on the inside
Sometimes I wonder what its like
To know my own reflection
To know who is looking back at me when I stand in front of the mirror.

The Reality of My Existence

Sitting in a room alone with my thoughts I wonder what's left of the person
I once was
I wonder what all remains the same as well as what has changed
Do I even remember who I use to be?
Did I ever really know who is me?
Sitting here my head pounding
Is the cause my mind or the others inside me?
Some days I cannot tell who it is looking at me through the mirror
Do I know who it is that stares back through that shard of reflective glass?
Why do I feel every emotion not just mine?
Why do I feel as if I'm losing my mind?
What is real and what is not?
Am I trapped inside an amber casing only thinking this is existing?
My mind pounds as if by unforgiving fists
My nose begins to bleed as if I was actually hit

Does my mind know something I don't- yet hides it like secrets untold?
Does my body still hide guilt and shame of things I did not choose from a
time before the concept of old entered my mind?
Do I still carry the wounds I thought had healed?
Do the scars that disappeared from my skin still stain my soul?
I know what happened was not my fault- I did not choose for it to unfold
Yet here I sit burdened with emotions I don't want to feel
And still most days I feel as if this is all a dream
I'm waiting to awake from a coma to my true reality
My childhood I spent in a haze
Always seeing myself in the mirrors of a clown house

Distorted pictures of myself
To many of me to even count
Stuck trapped in maze that was my mind
Always fighting to get outside
Outside my mind to the world of reality
I did not know there would never be an escape for me
The isolation I know doesn't help takes me by the hand and leads me back
into my mind
The only mind I can never escape is the one in charge of this race

A race I didn't sign-up to run
Yet I find my feet hitting the ground in a rhythm that does not suit my
current life
No matter the quality of my existence- my mind assures me I must live in
resistance
My whole life has been an attempt at a Houdini act
And now I have no need for this perfected act
Yet as soon as emotions intrude- my mind insists I must escape
To feel but to feel too much is still at times not feeling enough
Because feeling too much flips a switch in my mind and in the moment I'm
carried off

Carried off from the emotions that plague me
Ironically the emotions that remind me that this is reality
My mind refuses to allow me to exist in a world of emotions that could hurt
me
My mind never learned how to process or handle the hard emotions that
leave it with pain, fear, and countless tears
My eyes barely release a tear as they drown me on the inside
Tears weren't safe when I was young and now my mind assumes the same
I feel but I feel too much which also means I don't feel enough
Emotions stacked on top of emotions weigh me down until I'm overcome
by this familiar numb

A numb that becomes a tingling in my mind as if electric pulses at the tips
of thin needles are poking my brain
I feel this when there's to many emotions- I feel it when I'm at work
My mind screams out crying to escape as I enter into any public space
How does one live like this- wanting connection but fearing the human race
Perceived threats at every turn
Anxiety that overtakes when my wife is not right beside me
My wife is the only one that makes me feel completely safe
So when we're not sharing the same space- my mind attempts to yank me
away from the reality I try to stay tethered to
How do I find myself within my mind?
How do I stay present in the current time?
Does my mind not realize its not an escape?
When it pulls me inside itself in moments in reality that are quite and safe-
it forces me to relive flashes of unwanted memories
These memories that my mind cannot seem to erase
They are paired with the physical feelings that leave me scrubbing my own
skin off my body
I rarely sleep because when I close my eyes all I see is unwanted memories
All I feel is the touch and pain of what made me first feel shame
I attempt to stay awake until my body shuts off

Because if I try to sleep by closing my eyes I'm met with a silent film of
horrors lodged in my mind

Sometimes I do dream of things that seem to only make sense to me
Dreams that show what is to come and dreams with messages that feel like
my spirit had left my body to travel as soon as my eyes shut
But even those dreams cannot erase the nightmares of my existence that I
see when my eyes first shut
The nightmares that are the true horrors of my earliest realities
I sit alone my insides filling with tears
I just hope when I find the real me that they're not consumed by all those
nightmares

When I ask who am I really?
I fear the answer- what if I learn I'm just a shadow left behind of a life of constant nightmares?
What if I learn there truly is no escape from the horrors imbedded in my mind?
What if there's no way to escape the emotional brokenness?
Will I ever truly find rest?
When I die will I roam with the other spirits who are restless and unable to leave this plane of existence?
Will my mind ever feel like just a mind?
Or will it always feel like a maze inside?

I cannot bare the sight of who stares back at me in the mirror
Its as if the reflection in the glass represents me feeling trapped
When will living feel like life?
When will I not feel like I'm losing my mind?
Sometimes I imagine a different life- a life in a different time- a life as something else
A mere fantasy and nothing else
The books I used to read in efforts to escape reality now become the doors to the daydreams within my mind
The places I go in order to hide from the pain of memories lodged in my mind
Therapy it helps- but it only comes around once a week for one hour
Leaving me to try to cope with reality on my own the other 167 hours a week
Having to deal with crippling anxiety
Emotions that cut me deep- leaving my spirit out to bleed
I only ever learned how to run and fight
I never learned how to fully calm my mind
I feel like I'm screaming out for help
Crying until my insides flood and drown me out
Yet my mouth never opens
My voice never heard

My screaming can only be read because growing up speaking out was not
allowed
Speaking out posed to many threats that held the power to erase me from
existence completely
Now I cry silently anytime I have to ask for help because it makes me feel
inadequate and incompetent
I was told as a child I should be able to do everything on my own
As an adult now I know feeling alone eats away at my soul
Yet my mind refuses to easily allow for me to seek out help even of a basic
task
My mind further isolates me- distancing me from connections in reality
My mind questions who could or would ever fully love me
My mind tries to convince me that when someone wants to be alone its
because they cannot stand me
My mind tells me no one actually likes me or wants me around
So I push myself until I break hoping if I'm valuable enough I won't be
replaced
My mind it tells me I'm too much and won't allow me to fully open up
I'm afraid if try to talk about what feels like slowly dying on the inside that
everyone I love will leave my side
I fear I'll be the only one left that loves- that everyone else will lose the love
they say they have for me
I'm afraid to say it- that I'm struggling
I don't know how to answer the questions in their minds- I just know what I
feel inside

The things that should not bother or plague me anymore they still sit within
me and churn
This bitter butter made of memories I know is probably unhealthy- but its
too heavy to move on my own and my mind insists I must move it alone
I just want my mind to stop feeding me the lies from my broken childhood
I want my mind to heal not to escape
I want to exist in peace
Not forcing myself to keep a fast pace

I want my mind to feel safe to slow down
I want my mind to stop making me drown
The fears of my childhood plague my existence
I cannot even go into public spaces without feeling the need to scream in
fear- fear of horrors a stranger might inflict
Fear of being left by myself
Fear of being surrounded by people I have never met
The fear that consumes me every night I work before the store closes its
doors
Every time an unknown male walks by the fear consumes me on the inside
My mind it screams to run for safety
It says what if he to tries to rape me
Every time an unknown man walks past me- my heart sinks in my chest

My heart slows down as if to appear already dead

My anxiety spikes once he is out of sight
And I almost cry but realize I'm not in a place my mind perceives as safe- so
I clench my jaw and my mind begins to slip away
This is why I can't keep track of the distance of time while I'm at work
Because my mind pulls me into a place where I dissociate
I leave reality and I cry inside my mind
I realize I'm still terrified
The toll of being sexually and physically abused starting at the age of 2
It takes hold and seems to never let go
I just want to not be scared every time I'm out there
Every time I see a random guy- I don't want to automatically fear for my life
And my mind has asked countless times
"Why was I...?"
I just want to be able to be in public and not feel like I'm having a heart
attack every time an unknown man is near
To not feel like nearly slowly my heart to the point of death will make my
existence disappear
I know it won't make me invisible- but my mind is convinced

As if they are some version of Predator and only see heat waves

My mind draws me into isolation
Because it refuses to release the fears that at one time offered protection.

What She Felt Inside

It felt like a cavern of space was pushing its way between them
She didn't know why it felt this way it just did
She craved affection
She craved physical displays of love
She felt a sadness nah sorrow within herself
The sorrow felt as if it was warping her and weaving itself into her very soul
She felt the tears within but rarely did they show
She felt foolish for even feeling sorrow but her emotions belonged to their
selves
not her, she just existed within them not the other way around
She knew she was loved but sometimes just knowing doesn't stop the cavern
of
space from growing
Sometimes just knowing doesn't feel the same as her language of love being
spoken to her heart and soul
Most days she would sit waiting
Waiting to feel desired
Waiting to be drowned in affection
Because she didn't want to be overbearing
Or at times because she felt her displays of affection and adoration were
unwanted or shunned
At times it felt like casting a line into a fishless lake waiting for something to
grab
hold
Or like running towards something in sight that appears to constantly stay
the
same distance away regardless of how far she ran in its direction

Part of her the part where the sorrow had rooted itself within her felt like an
empty void
A void that wasn't being filled but a void that had at first not existed
A void from a past time which had first been filled to overflow but recently
drained empty
It was as if every time the void was filled and became a holding place for
what
she craved it grew to hold more and more as her heart's
and soul's needs/desires were met and exceeded
But it felt like one day the waterfall that once ran to fill this place became a
dew drop
And the space that had learned to grow to receive and hold what was filling
it
one day turned from feeling too small to feeling too large
This feeling left a void that led to a feeling of thickened air between them.

2, 8, 20, 23

I hear constant screams and uncontrollable crying day and night in the back
and at times at the front of my mind-
This young "me" stuck as a toddler, maybe she's the reason I've always felt
like I'll forever be a child-
The memory of my older brother doing what he wasn't supposed to do to
me,
I've always rationalized it as "he didn't know better, he was just a child too,
only doing to me what his mom's boyfriend was doing to him"-
But is that why looking back I realize the unhealthy attachment I had to
him?
My older brother-
It was if I was his shadow, always by his side whether following him around
or fighting with him-
So many things were wrong in my life at that time, but I didn't realize how
wrong that was.
This young "me" stuck as a toddler, maybe she's the reason I've always felt
like I'll forever be a child-
Flashbacks to being stuck in my room unable to get out while my mom was
at work and my dad sat in front of the tv idly playing video games, paying no
mind to the fact his children where in the other room cry and screaming to
get out, to eat, to drink, to have their diapers changed, to be loved and cared
for-
The sound of my mom being hurt by my dad in the other room not
knowing how to not hear it.
This young "me" stuck as an 8yr old, maybe she's the reason I feel like I have
to save everyone-

She was only 8yrs old when she had to start helping raise her younger
siblings, being "mom" to children she didn't bare-
That scared child who stood in front of flying fists and double-edged words
pretending to not be hurt because she had to be strong for everyone else and
hold everyone's worlds together-
She was the glue of the family even though she could barely hold herself
together she struggled to hold everyone and everything else together.
This young "me" stuck as an 8yr old, maybe she's the reason I feel like I have
to save everyone-
I hear this bright sweet young girl's voice in my mind try to explain the
unraveling of my mind to me like a mother would to her young child-
This little girl explains to me "I'm key-key's older sister. You spent so much
time wishing you had an older sister to protect you and be there for you
how you were for your younger siblings, so I'm here to protect key-key"-
I hear this and I want to cry as if this 8yr old girl is real and going through
the things I did.
This 20yr old "me", a guy swore to keep us from pain-
I hear his voice in my mind saying "You and key-key can't handle the
memories; you can't have them"
I remember messing around with someone I work with and one night
saying, "I'm just really off tonight, I had a nightmare that two guys got into
my apartment, and they were about to rape me
right before I woke up" and the guy looked at me and said, "That's an
unrealistic fear" AND with that I began to feel my mind slip-
That's when I started to become a passenger in my body, seeing and hearing
but rarely being able to participate though I fought to get out, out of my
own mind-
I vaguely remember the past 6 months, a new name, a new gender, a new
tattoo-
I look in the mirror and see a man or better yet a fearful boy who wants to
be the man that protects us like Papa did when Papa was still alive-
All I can feel is distress, I miss my femininity, my long hair, my delicate face
and sweet higher pitched voice that testosterone has now seemingly
distorted-

I feel like an awful parent, I barely remember the last 6 months with my
kids, I have to ask someone else questions on my kids' personalities and
milestone markers because I'm not completely aware of how to answer those
kinds of questions.
In the last 6 months I've lost so much it seems-
Memories-
Friendships-
Relationships-
My mind.
I now feel even more out of place-
Like I constantly want to cry and scream like key-key –
Have I become the broken little girl I was afraid of becoming? Or have we
always been the same person and I was just forced to pretend I was grown
up, forced to leave key-key behind locked up in the torcher chamber known
as my mind?
I feel alone even when surrounded by people-
I feel insane even though others say this is a perfectly normal response to
trauma-
I feel out of place like we're back to being an outcast or someone living a life
that doesn't belong to us-
We're lost and scared and trying to be a neurotypical human-
All while we're surrounded by broken pieces of our mind that's shattered
and scattered around the floor our reflections staring back at us asking who
we are –
These shards of broken memories beg to become the weapons we slit our
minds with forcing the pain to overtake forcing us to remember things we
forced ourselves to lock away-
In the physical realm suicide would result in the extinction of our existence,
but our minds beg for us to commit psychological suicide to let the
memories bleed out and to lay powerless in a sea of painful memories that
make us ask "why?"-
"Why we were created? Born? Forced to live through the things we did?"-
As we realize what it means to ask for what we ask for we realize that maybe
it's better off not to ask, but yet we want to be strong and face it all-

Our psyche trying to protect us by creating new names, new people within
our mind, each to serve a different purpose.
As we finish writing the words on this page, we see our body what's
supposed to be "my" body banging fists against a mirror standing in a pool
of our own tears trying to get out of our own minds-
Only one full length mirror blackness abyss on all other sides we're sure we
could escape if we tried but something or someone is holding us back
chaining our psyche from moving.
And in our minds, we're lost-
Always stuck as if unmoving-
2,8,20,23-
The ages we're left with staring at us trying to find their selves or trying to
pick up their brokenness find a way to fix, us-
2,8,20,23-
Why are we the ones our psyche left behind?

Dissociation of Time

The sands of time cascade down a man made vile
A construct created by man but not true to existence
I feel every moment from every point in what man calls time
Yet here I sit longing to break free
Wondering how to escape this cage they refrain us in from birth
As seconds, minutes, hours pass I wonder if I'm the only one who sees how
this imaginary thing dictates and controls the happenings of life
I know the deception because I at times escape it but commonly with no
memory of its absences.

Disconnect

Years of healing and it's not over,
I thought I had it under control, but the flashbacks come, and my mind
leaves me off and on throughout the night as I work,
I don't hear what others say,
I'm always asking "Huh?"
Or
"What?"
My thoughts are too loud the images too vivid
At times the disassociation overtakes, Sometimes it goes unnoticed by
others,
Sometimes it causes a stumble and I fall and hit the ground,
The eyes of worry burn my skin and the judgement crawls from their eyes
across my body I blame the fall on a slide of foot and turn up the music
filling my ears,
I don't hear the music that's playing its only there to blame when I'm
unaware of what's around me

At times like this its either nightmares in the day or my awareness fleeing by
night,

For some reason people constantly question "How are you?" always caring
when I never asked them to,
I don't understand why it's vital to feel like people care, Is it the logical
aspect of my autism?
Is it that I emotionally disconnect now?
I don't feel the need to form new friendships or relationships for that
matter-

303

I just merely exist in a world manipulated by thoughts of the white man-
This little native child has always felt disconnected-
Disconnected from their culture-
Disconnected from their people-
But worst of all disconnected for their self-
The feeling of disconnect worsens when I come to realize that I wasn't
present in my physical body-
Or the cultural and ancestral disconnect that comes with every native
comment,
"You're to white or light skinned to be native"
"You're not enrolled in a tribe"

"You can't speak any of the tribal languages from either side of your family"
"You've never been to a powwow"
"You haven't [this] so you can't be native"
The disconnect from comments like,
"Foster kids don't grow up and succeed, look at the statistics"
"Single parents always struggle"
"Working full time, having twin toddlers, and doing full time college, I
don't know how you'll manage"
Or how about the disconnect caused by guilt,
Maybe if I had told the doctors 'no' to the testing maybe my daughter
would've been born alive-
Maybe if I would've stuck through the depression my sister wouldn't have
become our adoptive mom's punching bag-
Maybe if I knew how to handle and cope with my feelings,
I could've had a successful relationship-
Maybe if I wasn't so scared of being sexually assaulted again,
I would be more comfortable being feminine-

Maybe if I could love who this body encases maybe then I wouldn't feel so
out of place-
Maybe I'm really the reason for the broken homes as a child-

I must be the reason for the broken dynamic my kids live with- I must be
what's wrong right?
I connect fine with my kids and anyone I met in 2012 or before-
But for some reason I can't fully connect or trust anyone new or anyone
who came into my life after 2012.

Unknown Approaching

Deep in the hollow bones of my soul a cry echoes out,
Some part of me that was buried nearly a lifetime ago.
I cannot tell if she is broken or lost,
Maybe fearful,
Something about the unknown awakens her.
As she claws to the surface her cries get louder,
The misunderstood creature from within.
How long has she been here?
No one truly knows,
Not even I.
She's not weak,
Just silent,
'til the unknown approaches.
Like creaking floorboards,
My insides bend under the weight of her ascending climb.
Like a child with no friends,
My mind wonders if she's here because of me.
Is it the unknown that calls to her,
Or the crawling of my skin that I feel as the fear of the unknown arises?
Am I her- this creature?
Is she me?
Is this creature the embodiment of my fears I locked away?
Is she more real than I?
Who am I if not this creature?
Who is this creature if not I?
Her cries eerie like a howl under a full moon's night,
Has she lingered deep within all these years?

Or is it that I do not hear her voice unless she unleashes a cry?
Is she my pain- my fear?
When I ignore those am I ignoring her?
Is she the truest piece of me?
She must be? Right?
The parts of me not seen by others,
The terrors from within my mind.
You would call her a beast,
Or a creature of the night.
But may it be,
To me she is not,
She is something else complete.
This creature from within,
She must be,
She is,
Pure emotions from inside me.
And yet,
I only sense her when the unknown approaches me.

The Table In My Mind

The thoughts, the insecurities, they build up refusing to leave
They make their selves known as they pull up seats to a table, they set
themselves
Uninvited they remain no matter how many times they're told to leave that
they're not welcome in my mind's company
They start out as if gossip whispered from ear to ear until they realize I'm
attempting to force them from their table then their voices start to rise, and
they get louder and louder until it's hard not to hear the things they say

"She'll change her mind"
"She'll realize you're not worth her time"
"She doesn't want to marry you; she only says she does to try to suffice you"

"Anyone who has ever promised you forever has always made excuses for
why they couldn't or rather wouldn't marry you, why would that ever
change you silly girl"

"You're too much to bear"

"You've always been a burden and hindered anyone you've been with, so
don't think for a second that that's not what you are now, a burden, a
hinderance"

"But don't tell her this is how you feel it'll just push her away, it'll just show
her how insecure you really are"

"Stop hoping for a happily ever after it will never come, you're a naive little girl who still believes in fairytales and who thinks this is one"

"Wake up and realize no matter how much you heal no matter how hard and deep you love, no matter what you do you'll never truly be enough, you'll never truly be worth anything, you've been through too much to be anything more than broken"

These thoughts, these insecurities they refuse to leave the table they've set for themselves
And in turn I feel pushed into silence as if nothing I say will matter anyways
And I know these thoughts, these insecurities are remnants from a childhood that turned me invisible and called me nothing more than a broken and lost child who will never amount to anything.

A Life With DID

How did no one know?
I knew.
Well I didn't know exactly what it was, but I knew something was wrong.
I knew other kids my age knew who they were
Other kids didn't erase their name 10 times because they couldn't get their
name right,
Other kids didn't get talked to by the teacher for writing the wrong name on
their assignments.
How did no one know?
I knew.
I knew I felt like I was trapped inside my head, beating on walls carved from
my brain.
I knew looking through my eyes felt like looking through a window seeing
another me inside my brain who saw another me looking out a window
while another me looked down on me and my other me(s) from a sky
within the head of yet another me.
I knew that thin fragile piece of glass mocked me as I searched it for a
reflection of someone I recognized.
How did no one know?
I knew.
I knew my days and weeks blurred together as if time didn't really exist,
I knew it felt like I left my body every time my dad took advantage of it,
I knew the girl others thought I was felt like she didn't exist,
I knew deep inside shackled in chains on a cement floor in my mind sat the
version of me who feared everyone and everything in sight.
How did no one know?
I knew.

I knew I felt like I was screaming for help but my voice never left my chest,
I knew I reported the abuse but when police came they questioned me in
front of my dad so I lied and said it never happened because he said he
would kill people I loved.
How did no one know?
I knew.
I knew I felt broken and shattered like my life was a series of glitches,
I knew I felt like who I was was constantly being altered,
I knew I erased where my name went until there was a whole in the paper,
I knew I didn't know me.
How did no one know?
I knew.
I knew something wasn't right within me,
Did no one care enough to see,
To see the shifting fragments of my reality,
To see the shifting fragments of my shattered psyche.
How did no one see me until I was grown and struggling?
Why was it only in therapy that someone finally saw me?
Saw the child that was beat and raped,
Saw the child left to fend for their self,
Saw the child that had to parent their parents while playing parent to 6
younger siblings.
Why did my dad say he knew what was going on?
Did he purposely cause these fragments to form?
Was my psyche some sick experiment or a twisted game?
Why did it take years of therapy to finally find a therapist who sees me as a
person and not as a problem?
Why did it take years to find a therapist that understands my psyche and all
of its fragmented versions of me?
How did no one know?
I knew
I know now.
I know now these fragments are shields constructed by my psyche-
Each a piece of the puzzle to who I am and the traumas I've faced,
I know now I'm not broken or shattered

I know now these feelings have a name,
Dissociative Identity Disorder that's the name,
DID is it to blame or is it to thank?
How did no one know?
I was a child and I knew something wasn't the same between me and other
kids my age.